Day Trading: Absolute Beginners Guide to Trading Cryptocurrency including Bitcoin, Ethereum & Altcoins

This book contains 2 manuscripts:

Cryptocurrency: The 10 Biggest Trading Mistakes Newbies Make - And How to Avoid Them

Cryptocurrency: 13 Coins to Watch with 10X Growth Potential in 2018

By Stephen Satoshi

Contents

Cryptocurrency: 13 More Coins to Watch with 10X Growth Potential in 2018

Financial Disclaimer:

I am not a financial advisor, these are my own opinions and the information contained within this book is not financial advice. This is not an investment guide nor investment advice. I am not recommending you buy any of the coins listed here. Any form of investment or trading is liable to lose you money.

There is no single "best" investment to be made, in cryptocurrencies or otherwise. Anyone telling you so is deceiving you.

There is no "surefire coin" - one again, anyone telling you so is deceiving you.

With many coins, especially the smaller ones, the market is liable to the spread of misinformation.

Never invest more than you are willing to lose. Cryptocurrency is not a get rich quick scheme.

"Men wanted for hazardous journey. Low wages, bitter cold, long hours of complete darkness. Safe return doubtful. Honor and recognition in event of success."

— Ernest Shackleton.

"Never confuse brains with a bull market"

— Anonymous.

Introduction

So you've decided to take the plunge into the cryptocurrency fast lane. You're looking for those gigantic returns you've read so much about. Well, you've come to the right place. Trading is without a doubt the quickest way to get rich with cryptocurrency.

From the outset though, let's make something clear. Trading is incredibly risky, and you are liable to lose money if you don't know what you're doing. The entire point of this book is avoid making giant mistakes, that losing traders always seem to make. So you can mitigate some of the risk by directing your attention to learning the right trading principles to set you up for long term trading success.

These aren't just technical principles, and I won't have you studying 500 chart patterns for 3 years before investing your first dollar, pounds or euros. There are significant mental preparations you need to make before you begin trading. This applies to cryptocurrencies, as well as any other financial trading situation. You'll also need to learn the principles of money management, and how to correctly use your bankroll to give you the biggest chance of long term trading success.

It is advisable to spend a significant portion of your time studying trading theory before you spend time trading your hard earned coins. Remember, at its very core, trading comes down to two factors, and two factors only.

1. Making money
2. Keeping what you've made

As we're currently in one of the biggest bull markets ever seen, many people are doing number one quite well. However, what remains to be seen is if they'll keep their money once the market turns bearish, and our beloved cryptocurrencies start to drop in price (which is a matter of when, and not if - this is a financial market after all).

Trading is the ultimate rush, it's a game played against one another via a computer screen, where it's your mind against another person, your money against theirs. Some days you come home a conquering hero, and other days you'll be left beaten, demoralized and broken. Hopefully, you'll be having more of the former than the latter after studying this book, and you'll become a consistently profitable trader going forward.

And as per usual: **Only invest what you can afford to lose**

I wish you all the best in your trading endeavors,

Stephen

Trading vs. Investing

For the vast majority of people, buying a coin and holding it for the long term is a smarter move than actively trading one or multiple coins at once. You see, cryptocurrency trading is rife with uninformed “traders” who simply buy and sell on a whim and inevitably end up broke, even in the current bull market conditions. Luckily for you, if you take some time to study the basics, you can outwit and outtrade these people and take consistent profits for yourself.

Trading Cryptocurrency vs. Big Board Stocks or Penny Stocks vs. Forex

If you’ve dabbled in trading securities before, then you’ll probably be familiar with some of the concepts discussed in this book. However, there are a few major differences between trading cryptocurrency and trading traditional stocks or even penny stocks.

The main one of these is that the cryptocurrency market is open 24/7 365. There are no weekends off, there are no market closures at 1PM for holidays or anything like that. As such, traditional trading advice such as “the best time of day to trade” falls by the wayside here. Price movements can happen while you sleep because the Chinese market is already up and trading, or there is a large volume of buy order coming in from Korea. Events like this aren’t uncommon, and you need to be aware of these factors before committing to trading.

Mistake 1: Falling for Pump & Dump Schemes

Opt-In Pump & Dump Emails

Another thing to be aware of. These are a hangover from the mid 2000s when penny stock trading was all the rage, and scammy stock promoters would send out emails to their list promoting a certain stock. Either because they were paid to do so by the company, or the promoters had already invested big themselves. They then wait for the email recipients to invest and push the price up even more, before dumping their shares on the market for a profit, leaving the email recipients holding large losses.

Unfortunately, due to the lack of regulation by the SEC, companies regularly do this for cryptocurrency as well. That is why I recommend you don't subscribe to any of these types of emails, whether a free or paid service. Your trading should be done based on market condition and technical analysis, which we'll go into in more depth later on in this book.

Technical Analysis

Mistake 2: Not utilizing technical analysis

Why Technical Analysis is vital in any form of financial trading

1. Future trends follow past trends

Human beings are a predictable bunch, and we generally do the same things over and over again. This also applies to trading, because certain patterns emerge and repeat themselves, and we can use the patterns to somewhat accurately predict price movements.

2. We’re all looking at the same charts

Individual human beings are less good at predicting things than a group of humans predicting the same event, the "wisdom of the crowd" if you will. How this relates to cryptocurrency trading is that as there are thousands of us looking at the same chart, we will generally come to the same conclusion and make similar moves to one another.

3. The current cryptocurrency price includes all available data

Even data that isn't widely or publicly available will be factored in (this is the advantage that so-called "insiders") have over the rest of the trading population. Thus, we can assume that the current price of the cryptocurrency is correct.

All technical analysis can be broken down into 2 main chart patterns:

Continuation Patterns - Where the price of a coin is expected to keep trending the same way it is currently moving

Reversal Patterns - Where the price of a coin is expected to reverse from its current trend (I.e. a coin's price is expected to stop falling and start rising)

The following are some of the basic, and most essential chart patterns you need to know. You can get by with an in-depth knowledge of these, and having a deeper knowledge of the basics charts is better than having surface level knowledge of many charts.

For more in-depth reading on technical analysis, I having a recommended reading list at the end of this book.

Support & Resistance

If you're going to learn one technical tool for trading, make it support and resistance levels. These horizontal trend lines are the lifeblood of all technical analysis.

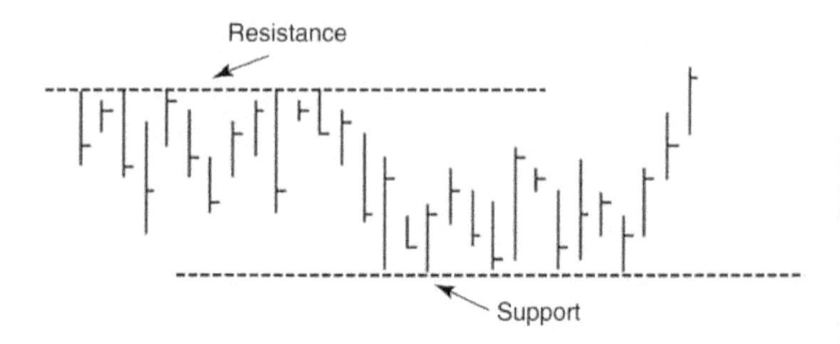

Support Level:

A support level for a coin is a price in which traders do not think it will fall below. They believe there is enough demand at that price that investors will continue to buy, and this will prevent any further declines in the price. Support levels can be identified using charting patterns.

If you're just starting out, study longer term historical data and use this to identify previous support levels for a coin. So with the case of Bitcoin, use 6 month or 12 month graphs rather than 1 week graphs.

Resistance Level:

Resistance level is simply the opposite of a support level. It's a price where traders don't believe there is enough demand to break through and go higher, therefore more traders will be selling at this particular price. Resistance levels are calculated slightly differently than support levels due to the nature of human psychology. For example, round numbers often have a psychological effect e.g. Bitcoin @ $10,000 or ETH @ $300 and this creates a resistance level in itself.

You can also use the reverse of the techniques you used to find a support level on a chart.

For both support and resistance levels, look for at least two or three price action zones in a single chart. Once you identify this price action zones, you can draw a straight line to indicate support and resistance levels. Generally speaking, the more a coin hits a specific support or resistance level, the stronger the price move will be once it does finally break through.

Once a stock breaks through it's resistance level, it's not uncommon for the previous resistance level to become the new support level and vice versa. Understanding this helps your risk management as you continue to trade more frequently.

Candlestick Charting

Candlestick charting, also called Japanese candlesticks is one of the best ways to determine support and resistance levels in a coin. Candlesticks take into account the opening, closing, high and low price of that particular day for a coin.

There are literally hundreds of different candlestick patterns you can learn, but there are a few that are absolutely vital to know, so those will be the ones we discuss in this book. One more thing to point out when studying candlestick charts. Red or black candlesticks represent downward movement, whereas white or green candlesticks represent upward movement.

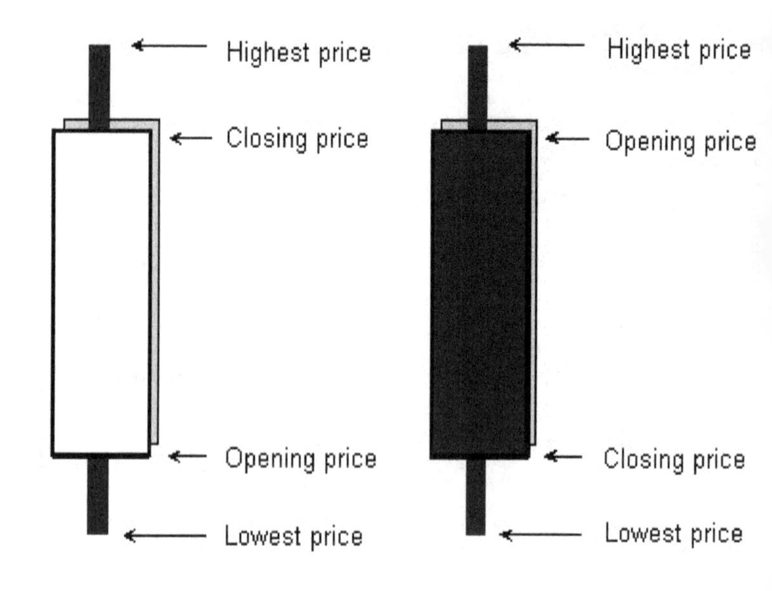

Doji

Doji's are characterized by a very small difference between opening and closing price and look like plus signs on a chart. The Doji pattern represents indecision in the market, these are usually found near support and resistance points, because market participants aren't sure if the coin will break these levels.

When analyzing candlestick charts, you should use daily charts that go back at least 3 months and try to identify patterns.

Channels

Channels are plotted with 2 parallel lines on a candlestick or line chart and denote continued support and resistance levels as a coin is trending in upwards or downwards fashion. Channels are useful because they help us form multiple ideal entry and exit points for a particular coin going forward. This is a big plus if you plan on trading frequently.

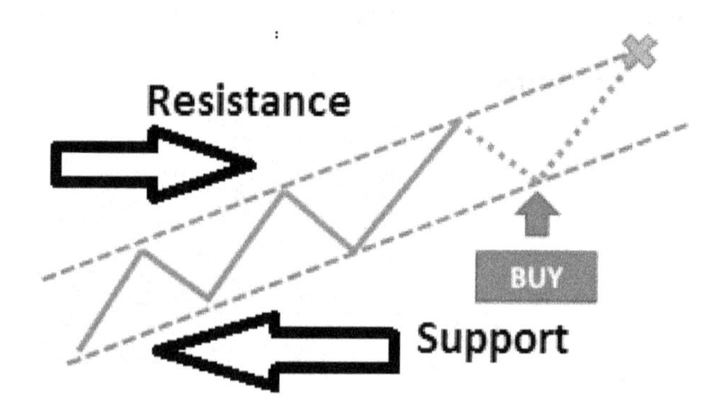

Head & Shoulders Pattern

One of the most important patterns to recognize is the head and shoulders reversal pattern. Simply put this indicates that the trend of the coin is about to reverse. So in the example below, the price is expected to drop. If the chart is inverted, we would expect a rise in price going forward.

The expected price movement (denoted by m in the picture) can be calculated as the inverse of the price between the neckline and the head, which is why it is crucial that you measure the neckline correctly.

Note, the majority of the time, the chart will not be a perfectly aligned head and shoulders, but the general pattern is enough to go on.

Head and Shoulder Top
Head
Left shoulder
Right shoulder
Price
Neckline
Period & volume

Double Top & Double Bottom

A double top (bearish), and its inverse the double bottom (bullish), are made up of 2 consecutive peaks with a trough in-between. Most of the time the first peak will be slightly higher than the second peak and be accompanied by a higher volume as well.

It is also not uncommon for there to be a triple top or triple bottom pattern if there is not enough volume to break through resistance or support levels. Like most patterns, once a breakthrough occurs, the previous support level becomes the new resistance level and vice versa.

The double top is one pattern that newer traders often misinterpret, especially when looking at short term charts. Remember to focus on volume at the support/resistance levels before entering a trade.

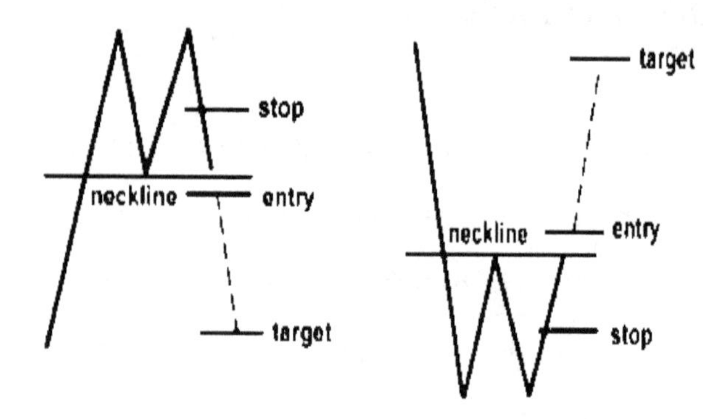

Double Top and Double Bottom

Triangles

We could probably write an entire book

just on various triangle based patterns, but we'll stick to the basics here. The three types of triangle pattern are the symmetrical, ascending and descending triangle.

Symmetrical Triangle

A symmetrical triangle is a continuation pattern that signals a price is going to keep moving in the same direction after a brief trend reversal. The two points of the triangle start from the support and resistance lines then converge. The price of the coin has been trading between these two lines and then will continue to trend in the previous direction once these lines meet.

Ascending Triangle

An ascending triangle is a bullish pattern that signals the price will keep moving upwards after a period of bouncing around the resistance line, but not dipping low enough to hit the support line. The line is drawn from the previous resistance and support lines, and will converge at the resistance line. If there is enough volume, the price will break the resistance line and continue to rise.

Descending Triangle

The opposite of the ascending triangle is a bearish pattern, except this time the lines converge at the support level. Enough volume at this level will result in a breakthrough to lower prices.

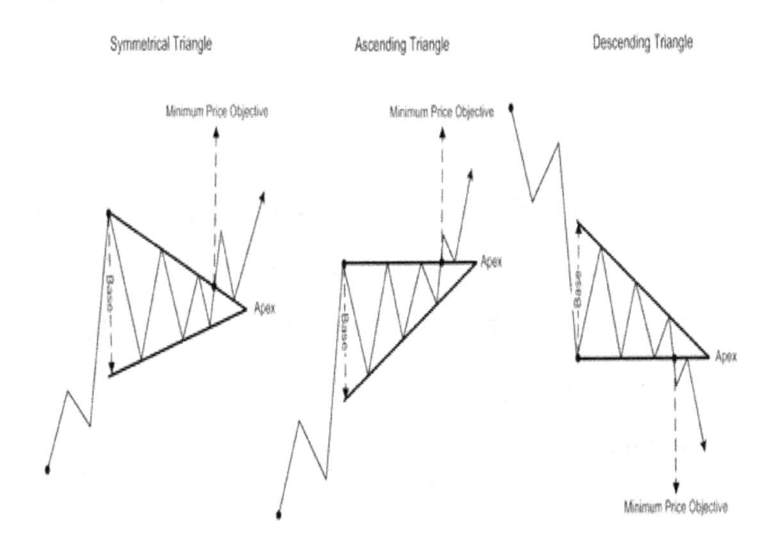

Flag Patterns

Flag patterns are similar to triangle patterns that appear during consolidation period (small reversal from previous price movements). They are represented by two parallel lines following a of a sharp price movement (which acts as the flag "mast") Following a flag patterns, prices continue to trend in the same direction they were moving previously.

The slope of the flag will be the opposite direction to the predicted price movement, so a downward sloping flag will signal a continued bull movement, and an upward sloping flag will signal a continued bear movement.

Like triangle patterns, the buy or sell signal comes when there is enough volume to break through the previous support or resistance level.

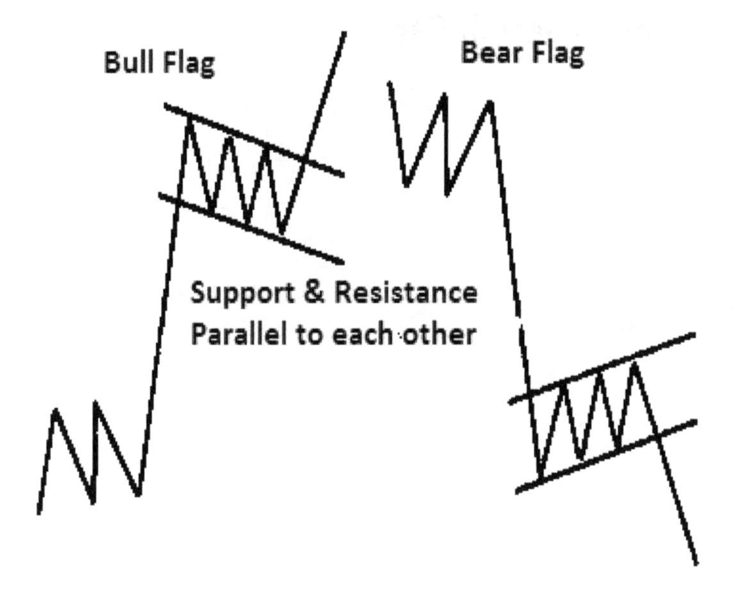
Bull Flag
Bear Flag
Support & Resistance
Parallel to each other

The Baseball Cap

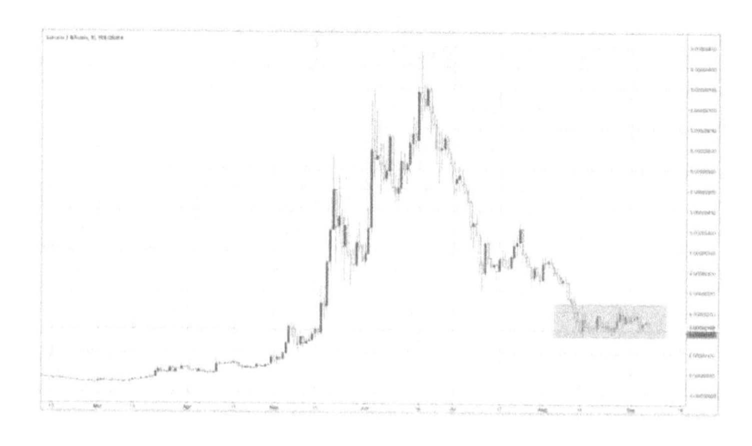

The Baseball cap is a consolidation pattern where a new support level forms after a dip in price. This new "floor price" means the price has stabilized for the time being, and due to the cyclical and high volatility nature of cryptocurrencies, this is usually followed a sharp increase in price. Like in the chart below. If you study the baseball cap pattern enough, then you can time you buys correctly - and therefore if you're going to learn one pattern well - make it this one.

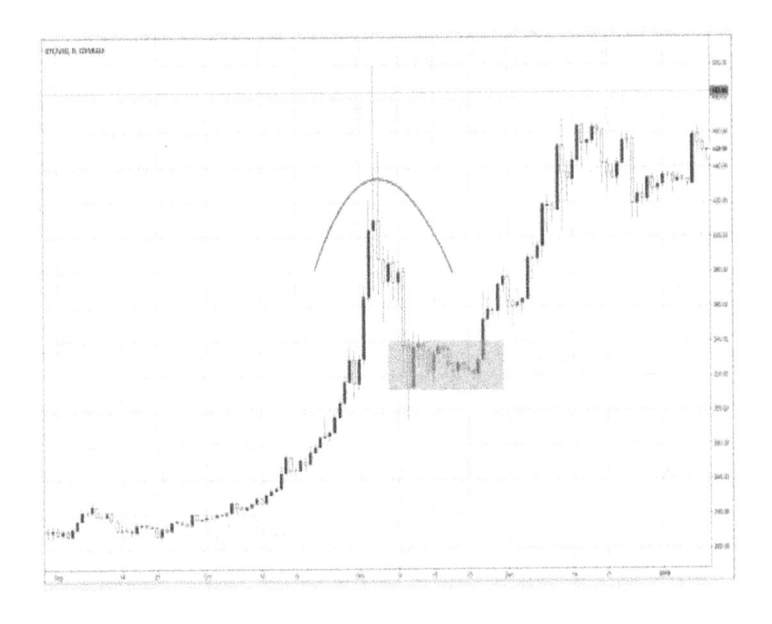

Trading Volume

Mistake 3: Not factoring volume into technical analysis

Another technical factor to take into account is the trading volume at a particular point in the chart. Ideally we want to see significant volume for upward trends, and lower volume for downward trends. If we see a downward trend accompanied by large volume, we can assume that this is not a weak trend and the price will continue to fall. Similarly, if we see volume is steadily decreasing on an upward trend, then this trend is likely coming to an end in the near future.

Limitations of Technical Analysis

Technical Analysis is just one tool that a trader needs in his arsenal. It is absolutely not the be all, end all of trading. Think of it as a guideline to making money, rather than a direct pathway.

The biggest factor is that we just don't have that much data available on the cryptocurrency market. Bitcoin has only been trading for 7 years now, and most other cryptocurrencies for less than 3. Unlike stocks where we have data for tens of years for individual stocks and the market as a whole.

Sometimes, if you dive too deep into the technical side of trading, you lose your instincts and even your common sense. Even if your charts are saying hold, you should probably sell if your position is up 100% over the past 3 days. After all, what goes up, must come down. Developing solid trading instincts is something that does take time, but the more trades you make, you'll start to subconsciously notice things.

Remember, if you are unsure of a trade based on your analysis, look at the bigger picture and add another timeframe to your chart to see if the same patterns emerge.

Trading Mindset/Trading Psychology

One of the biggest hurdles new traders have to overcome is acquiring the mindset of a successful trader. This is even more prevalent in the cryptocurrency market because its sheer volatility allows the potential for large losses in addition to large gains. These losses can be demoralizing for even seasoned pros, but the important thing to remember is to know that these losses will come (professionals estimate a 55:45 win/loss ratio for even the best traders), and how to deal with them when they do happen.

Acquiring a successful mindset is the single most important skill a trader must possess. Moreso than any technical tools. We must remember that we as humans have our own built-in biases, and even delusions, and many of these will hamper our trading ability. So the following is a list of important mindset and trading psychology factors that you must be aware of if you're going to become a successful trader.

Why Paper Trading is Useless

For years now, common trading advice has been that you should paper trade (trade with fake money) to get a hang of reading charts and learning when to buy and sell. However, I think this advice is limited at best, and potentially harmful.

You need to make mistakes with real money on the line, and you need to learn from these mistakes. Your brain and emotions simply don't react the same way if you know, deep down, that any losses you make are just on paper. To put it simply. You need to lose money to truly find out if trading is for you.

From then on, it's up to you how you react to these losses. Are you freaking out and trying to recoup them as soon as possible? Are you up until 4AM trying to get back some of the previous day's lost cash? If the answer is yes, then trading probably isn't for you. However, if you can accept that everyone has bad days, and learn to analyze your mistakes and decipher where exactly you went wrong, and most importantly, learn from them - you may well wind up as a successful trader in the long run.

Paralysis by Analysis

So, you've spent your time reading and studying charts, now it's time to go to CEX.io or your preferred trading website and deposit money into your account. So you do so, and begin looking at charts, and waiting...and waiting...but you just can't seem to pull the trigger. This happens to a lot of new traders, especially those who are naturally risk averse. You want everything to go perfectly and you want to start out on a good note. However, this is trading, and as previously mentioned, you need to make mistakes in order to get better.

This is also why you need proper money management in trading, because say you lose on 8 out of your first 10 trades (not uncommon by any means), you'll need to have properly managed your bankroll in order to be able to fight another day.

Knowing when not to trade

Mistake 4: Trading for the sake of trading

One of the more important qualities of a good trader is restraint. In other words, being able to understand that there are days where you don't need to make a trade. Maybe there are no obvious patterns appearing, maybe it's just a slow day in the market. Either way, you need to learn to take days off. This is good for preventing trading burnout as well, especially in the cryptocurrency market that is 24/7.

Accepting that the market is always right

One of our great cognitive biases as human beings, is believing we are better than we are at certain things. For example, are you an above average driver? I bet 90% of people will answer yes, but statistically, only 50% of people can be above average at anything, that includes trading as well.

What I'm getting at, is we often make excuses for our bad trades, such as the old classic "the market is wrong." The market will move in ways you don't expect, and if anyone had figured out a way to truly predict market direction, they would be a retired trillionaire by now. Your technical analysis will not influence the market, it will only help you make better decisions.

Accepting that you are wrong

Following on from the above point. The market isn't wrong, you are. You need to be able to accept that you will be wrong on many trades, even multiple trades in a row. Remember, judge yourself by your results, and not on any perceived "clever moves" you may have made. You will always have losers, but you need to be able to take a step back and accept this in order to move forward.

Taking Intermediate Profits

If your profits are only on paper, you haven't made squat. You need to convert some of your gains back to fiat from time to time. Taking profits helps you mitigate your need to even more money on paper, which leads to greed taking over, which inevitably leads to losing money in the long run. If you enter a trade at $70, with a plan to exit at $80 because you see resistance there, then exit at $80. Don't let the coin go to $80 and then revise your plan and hope it goes to

$100. There is no greater force that turns winning trades into losers, than that of greed.

Survivorship Bias

In my original book *Cryptocurrency: Beginners Bible* I talked about survivorship bias, and how seemingly everyone had made money with cryptocurrency. Well this is because winners speak up, and losers stay quiet. If you spend any time in the trading community, you'll be constantly surrounded by stories from traders who turned $300 in $50,000 in just a few weeks. Or a 19 year old kid from Russia who made $200 million in under a year. Of course success stories exist, but there doesn't mean there aren't as many, and in the case of trading, even more silent parties who lost money trading cryptocurrency. So the lesson here is to only measure yourself against yourself. If you're making continuous profits, then you're doing something right.

Recency Bias

You're only as good as your last trade is something that many traders suffer from, especially if they have a run of losers. This leads to negative mental energy, and a loss of confidence in oneself. What you need to learn to do, is not focus on these losses, but look at the bigger picture. Instead of focusing on your next trade, focus on your next 100 trades. By focusing on the next 100 trades, you remain committed to your trading fundamentals as opposed to chasing short term results and dopamine hits.

How to buy Cryptocurrency

Assuming you don't currently own any cryptocurrency, you'll need to buy some before you begin trading. The following is the most beginner friendly exchange for anyone looking to buy Bitcoin, Ethereum or Litecoin in exchange for fiat currency.

Coinbase

Coinbase represents the most simple way to buy Ethereum for those living in the US, Canada, the UK and Australia, in exchange for your local fiat currency. Based out of the US and regulated by the SEC, Coinbase is undoubtedly the most trustworthy cryptocurrency exchange out there today. Rates are competitive with the other major cryptocurrency exchanges, and the verification requirements are solid without being a hassle.

Currently Coinbase supports both wire transfers and purchases by debit and credit card. Once you signup for a Coinbase account and verify your ID, you can buy Ethereum, along with Bitcoin and Litecoin, instantly with your debit or credit card.

You can also store your cryptocurrency in Coinbase's vault system. If you do this, you will have to pass 2 factor authentication in order to spend it. This is one step more secure than simply leaving it on the exchange, but still is not as secure as offline storage option such as MyEtherWallet.

Another advantage of Coinbase is that they have a fully functional mobile app that allows the buying and selling of cryptocurrency on the go.

Now, as a special bonus to you - if you sign up for Coinbase using this link, you will receive $10 worth of free Bitcoin after your first purchase of more than $100 worth of Bitcoin, Ethereum or Litecoin.

http://bit.ly/10dollarbtc

Once you have purchased your Ethereum, there are a number of other exchanges I recommend if you want to trade Ethereum, many smaller cap cryptocurrencies do not allow for direct exchanges with fiat currency like USD, so you'll have to buy Bitcoin or Ethereum from Coinbase first, then exchange that for the other cryptocurrencies.

7 Common Cryptocurrency Trading Myths

Mistake 5: Believing any of these myths

1. **Cryptocurrency Trading Isn't Regulated therefore isn't safe**

This is one of the oldest cryptocurrency myths that still lingers around the market today. Cryptocurrency trading may not be regulated in the same way traditional securities trading is, but that doesn't mean the exchanges don't follow regulations. Coinbase and GDax are both registered in the United States and therefore need to comply with SEC guidelines. Other exchanges need to comply with their local jurisdictions as well.

2. **You need to know everything about blockchain technology to trade cryptocurrency**

Knowing the ins and outs of the coin you're trading might be helpful, but it's certainly not essential. In fact, an argument could be made that it is more beneficial *not* to know that much about your coin, to avoid making an emotional attachment.

Keeping up to date on cryptocurrency market news as a whole is advisable however. The two best sources for unbiased cryptocurrency news are.

http://coindesk.com

http://cointelegraph.com

3. **You need to know every single chart pattern every recorded**

You'd be much better off knowing the basics well, then having a broad but limited knowledge of hundreds and hundreds of different chart patterns. This is especially true when starting out, as you'll start to see patterns everywhere, even when they really aren't there, and as a result - make poor trades.

4. **Leaving your coins on an exchange is perfectly safe**

Exchanges are centralized, and therefore, are vulnerable to security exploits and hacks. From Mt. Gox in 2014 (which was handling 70% of the world's bitcoin transactions at the time) to Bitfinex in 2016, exchange hacks do happen. It's best to transfer any funds you are not using at the time to a safe, offline storage solution like a paper or hardware wallet.

5. You should follow one person/one source's cryptocurrency trading tips

Following a single person's advice is a good way to lose money, even if that person themselves is profitable, because there will be a delay in their trades and your trades. This means your margin will be lower, and thus you are less likely to make consistent profits over time.

A compounding factor to this is paid trading advice or paid newsletter subscriptions. These are often nothing more than pump and dump schemes by those running them. Unfortunately, as much of the cryptocurrency world is still unregulated, these schemes often go unpunished.

6. You should try to hit a home run with every trade

An important part of trading is knowing *when* to take profits. The newbie trader often mistakes the critical mistakes of going for just that extra 1 or 2% more, which often never appears and suddenly your gains have quickly turned into losses.

7. You can act as a perfect trader if you just learn the fundamentals

Unfortunately, as humans we have these little things called emotions. Fear, excitement, greed, all of these play a big part in our trading mindset and our subsequent trading actions. Mastering your emotions is a huge part of being a successful trader, and we'll look into this in more depth later on this book in the trading mindset and trading psychology section.

Best Cryptocurrency platforms for traders

Cex.io or http://bit.ly/cexsatoshi

With trading fees ranging between 0.1% and 0.2% per trade, CEX.io has some of the lowest fees in the crypto trading sphere. An added bonus on zero deposit fees for bank transfers and cryptocurrency deposits makes this a favorite among crypto traders.

Bitfinex

Bitfinex offers the best liquidity of any cryptocurrency exchange on the market today. They also offer margin trading. Their fees are slightly higher than Cex.io, and the tiers needed to access lower fees are also higher.

But Bitfinex still remains one of the premier cryptocurrency exchanges for trading today.

GDax

GDax is a subsidiary of Coinbase, so falls under the same SEC regulations a Coinbase does. The ease of transfers from Coinbase to GDax make it preferable to those who would rather keep their funds all on one single web ecosystem. Fees are slightly higher than both Cexio and Bitfinex, but the ease of transfers may outweigh these higher fees for some traders. GDax fees range from 0.1% to 0.25% for “takers” (buyers) 0% fee for “makers” (sellers).

Poloniex

Poloniex offers a wider range of cryptocurrencies than other exchanges listed here. So if you’re looking at trading some lower cap altcoin pairs, then Poloniex might be the best option for your trading.

Coinigy

Based out of Wisconsin, Coinigy is a rather interesting concept in that it's not an exchange itself. But a desktop application that gives you access to 45 different cryptocurrency exchanges from a single account. They also have 75 different technical indicators available. Although the interface might be overwhelming at first for new traders, more experienced traders may enjoy the sheer range of options available. Their pro account costs $15/month and allows for unlimited trading with no additional fees, which is extremely cheap if you plan on trading at high volumes. They also have an Android app if you want to trade on the go. At $15/month the expense is worth it, even for a novice trader because the charting features by themselves are extremely helpful if you're just starting out.

Mistake 6: Trading on the Wrong Exchange

Where not to trade cryptocurrency

You should stay away from any exchanges that could potentially be closed down by government regulators, these include Chinese exchanges. I would also not recommend Coinbase for trading, as the fees are higher than the other exchanges listed, however for a first time buyer, Coinbase is still the most accessible cryptocurrency exchange.

Where to store your cryptocurrency - Wallets & Cold Storage

Mistake 7: Storing your cryptocurrency on an exchange

Once you've successfully bought some cryptocurrency, be it Bitcoin, Ethereum or another altcoin, you'll need somewhere to safely store it.

Your cryptocurrency wallet is akin to a regular fiat currency wallet in the sense that you can use it to spend money, in addition to seeing exactly how much money you have at any given time.

However cryptocurrency wallets differ from fiat currency wallets because of the technology behind how the coins are generated.

As a reminder, the way the technology works means your cryptocurrency isn't stored in one central location. It is stored within the blockchain. This means there is a public record of ownership for each coin, and when a transaction occurs, the record is updated.

You can store your cryptocurrency on the exchange where you bought it like Coinbase or Poloniex, it is advisable not to do this for a number of reasons.

1. Like any online entity - these exchanges are vulnerable to hacking, no matter how secure they are - or what security measures they take. This happened with the Mt. Gox exchange in June 2011

2. Your passwords to these exchanges are vulnerable to keyloggers, trojan horses and other computer virus type programs
3. You could accidentally authorize a login from a malicious service like coinbose.com (example) instead of coinbase.com

Cold storage refers to any system that takes your cryptocurrency offline. These include offline paper wallets, physical bearer items like physical bitcoin or a USB drive. We will examine the pros and cons of each one.

Cryptocurrency wallets have two keys. A public one, and a private one. These are represented by long character strings. For example, a public key could be 02a1633cafcc01ebfb6d78e39f687a1f0995c62fc95f51e ad10a02ee0be551b5dc - or it could be shown as a QR code. Your public key is the address you use to receive cryptocurrency from others. It is perfectly safe to give your public key to anyone. Those who have access to you public key can only deposit money in your account.

On the other hand, your private key is what enables you to send cryptocurrency to others. For every transaction, the recipient's public key, and the sender's private key are used.

It is advisable to have an offline backup of your private key in case of hardware failure, or data theft. If anyone has access to your private key, they can withdraw funds from your account, which leads us to the number one rule of cryptocurrency storage.

The number one rule of Cryptocurrency storage: Never give anyone your private key. Ever.

Therefore, with your trading funds, it's advisable to keep any excess funds offline, a hardware wallet is an ideal way to do this because unlike a paper wallet, it is much simpler to transfer your funds between the hardware wallet and your computer in order to fund your trading account.

Paper Wallets:

Paper wallets are simply notes of your private key that are written down on paper. They will often feature QR codes so the sender can quickly scan them to send cryptocurrency.

Pros:

- Cheap - all you need a printer and some paper
- Your private keys are not stored digitally, and are therefore not subject to cyber-attacks or hardware failures.

Cons:

- Loss of paper due to human error
- Paper is fragile and can degrade quickly in certain environments

- Not easy to spend cryptocurrency quickly if necessary - not useful for everyday transactions

Recommendations:

It is recommended you store your paper wallet in a sealed plastic bag to protect against water or damp conditions.

If you are holding cryptocurrency for the long-term, store your paper inside a safe deposit box.

Ensure you read and understand the step-by-step instructions before printing any paper wallets.

Bitcoin:

http://bitaddress.org

http://bitcoinpaperwallet.com

Ethereum & ERC 20 tokens:

http://myetherwallet.com/

Litecoin:

https://liteaddress.org/

Hardware Wallets

Hardware wallet refer to physical storage items that contain your private key. The most common form of these are encrypted USB sticks.

These wallets use two factor authentication or 2FA to ensure that only the wallet owner can access the data. For example, one factor is the physical USB stick plugged into your computer, and the other would be a 4 digit pin code - much like how you use a debit card to withdraw money from an ATM.

Pros:

- Near impossible to hack - as of the time of writing, there have been ZERO instances of hacked hardware wallets

- Even if your computer is infected with a virus or malware, the wallet cannot be accessed due to 2FA
- The private key never leaves your device or transfers to a computer, so once again, malware or infected computers are not an issue
- Can be carried with you easily if you need to spend your cryptocurrency
- Transactions are easier than with paper wallets
- Can store multiple addresses on one device
- For the gadget lovers among you - they look a lot cooler than a folded piece of paper

Cons:

- More expensive than paper wallets - starting at around $60
- Susceptible to hardware damage, degradation and changes in technology

- Different wallets support different cryptocurrencies
- Trusting the provider to deliver an unused wallet. Using a second hand wallet is a big security breach. Only purchase hardware wallets from official sources.

The most popular of these are the Trezor (bit.ly/GetTrezorWallet) and Ledger Nano S wallets. For altcoins that are not supported by these wallet, you can create your own encrypted USB wallet by following online tutorials.

Money Management while trading

Mistake 8: Not having a money management game plan

One of the most overlooked, but undoubtedly most important skills while trading is learning how to manage your bankroll.

You can think of trading cryptocurrency as akin to playing poker in this respect. If you put 50% of your holdings into one hand, then it only takes 2 losing hands in a row to wipe you out.

What's more is, when you lose money, you need to make more on your next trade in order to get back to your initial position. For example, if you lose 50% on one trade, you need to make 100% back on your next trade to break even. That's why trading with only a small amount of your holdings on a single trade is the smart way to go.

So no, you should never go "all in" on one single trade, no matter how much of a sure thing you think it is. The higher % of your total holdings you use for an individual trade, the higher your overall risk. In fact, the reason so many traders is that they don't anticipate losing a number of trades in a row. The holds true no matter how good you are at identifying chart patterns, or any other learned trading skill. Without proper money management, you will eventually go broke.

So let's just numbers. Because of the high risk element of trading cryptocurrency, I personally recommend that you do not risk more than 1-2% of your account on a single trade. The more active trades you are making at one time, the lower risk per trade should be. When you are starting out, I advise you risk no more than 0.5% of your account for your initial trades. This sounds low, but big dips do happen, and these can add up quickly, therefore we want to lower our risk as much as possible.

One more thing, cryptocurrency trading is a cash only undertaking. Under no circumstances should you borrow money from family, friends or financial institutions to trade. You don't want to start your trading career already owing people money, this has a huge negative effect on your state of mind and will cause you to make bad trades.

Risk/Reward Ratio

This is a vitally overlooked factor in trading. As we previously mentioned, if you lose 50% on one trade, you have to make up 100% on the next trade in order to break even. Therefore, you should enter all trades with a reward:risk ratio of at least 2:1. In other words, you must expect to make at least twice what you are willing to lose on the trade, because this will cover your losses from losing trades in the future. For example, if you are willing to lose $100 on a trade, you must be trying to gain $200 from that same trade. A higher reward:risk ratio allows you to have more losing trades, because your higher profits from winning trades make up for your losses on losing ones.

How many trades should you have open at once?

This is largely dependent on how much time you can spend looking at charts per day, but generally, you shouldn't have more than 5 or 6 open trades at a time. When you're starting out then one or two will be enough to cause your brain to work overtime. Remember to set stop losses if you want to manage multiple trades at once.

Which cryptocurrencies should you trade?

That's entirely up to you, however you should beware of coins with very low market caps and liquidity levels, as these are more susceptible to market manipulation and organized pump and dumps from nefarious parties.

I would recommend everyone start out with Bitcoin, purely because the market has the most liquidity.

Keeping a Trading Journal

Now, I'm not talking about a trading diary where you complain about your week's trading woes. I'm talking about logging your trades in an excel spreadsheet or a google doc. You can learn so much just from looking at your past trades, and you'll learn a hell of lot more from your losers than you will your winners.

As a thanks for downloading this book, I've including a handy trading journal for you to log you trades.

You can download the free spreadsheet at http://bit.ly/SatoshiTradingSpreadsheet

What causes price movements?

We have to remember here, that we are trading cryptocurrencies and not traditional stocks, and as such, the metrics for determining price are different.

The big difference is that there is limited fundamental analysis we can do on a coin when compared to traditional stocks. For example, we don't have earnings reports to look at or quarterly profit/loss statements. We also don't have to be concerned with potential mergers occurring between cryptocurrencies. Apart from, having a working product already, how fast the transaction fees are and scalability of the project, there really isn't much in the way of fundamental analysis. Both of these factors are more important for long term investing than they are for short term trading.

Market Sentiment

Overall market factors play strongly in the growth of individual cryptocurrencies. We are dealing with a singular market after all. For example, when Mt. Gox was hacked in 2014, and 850,000 Bitcoin were stolen, the entire market dropped as a result.

The second part of this equation is how mainstream media often misreports cryptocurrency price movements, being all too quick to cite a “plunge” or “crash”. It’s now getting to the report where media reports citing a “crash” happen on days where the price is still UP over the previous 24 hours.

Bitcoin’s network effect is now so strong that many mainstream sources see Bitcoin as the be all, end all of cryptocurrency. Remember, buy the rumor, sell the news.

Bitcoin's price

The cryptocurrency market is still largely in its infancy, and as such, news regarding Bitcoin still greatly affects the market as a whole. At the time of writing, Bitcoin makes up roughly 56% of the overall cryptocurrency market cap, so any major Bitcoin price movements are reflected in the market as a whole. So even if you're trading smaller altcoins, it's wise to keep tabs on the price of Bitcoin as well.

Some commentators make the claim that Bitcoin and altcoin prices are inversely related, so if Bitcoin goes up, altcoins go down and vice versa. Whilst there is some data that backs up this theory, it isn't the entire story.

99% of people's first entry to the cryptocurrency market is into Bitcoin, this is even more so for institutional traders who move into cryptocurrency, because Bitcoin has the most liquidity, and therefore is an attractive market to enter. Therefore new money coming into the market is usually followed by investors moving their funds from altcoins into Bitcoin.

Asia

Mistake 9: Overlooking Asia' influence on the markets

One area to watch from looking for news to potentially affect trades, is any news coming out of Asia, particularly China and South Korea. These two countries have the highest volume of trades between them, more so than the USA, despite investors having to pay a premium (many South Korean exchanges trade cryptocurrencies for between 8-10% higher than

US or European based ones). Any government clampdowns on exchanges or changes in legislation regarding cryptocurrency, is bound to have a negative effect on price. An example of this was the temporary ban on Chinese citizens investing in ICOs, which caused market prices to drop sharply. This was further compounded by the South Korean Financial Services Commission taking the same steps.

Stop Loss/Stop Limit Orders

Mistake 10: Not utilizing stop loss/stop limit orders

Stop loss and stop limit orders are both risk management tools that allow you to both prevent excessive losses on a trade, and also lock in any unrealized profits on an open trade. Both of these are relatively simple tools, but you would be amazed by just how many traders (usually the unsuccessful ones) fail to use them in their trading strategy,

A stop loss order is a level or particular price you set to automatically sell your position in a stock, or in this case a coin. For example, if you buy Bitcoin at $1000, you can set a stop loss order at $900, so that if the price falls to $900, you will automatically sell your position at that level, providing there is enough liquidity to fulfill it.

To use the second example above, say you make the same buy order for Bitcoin at $100, but it then increases to $110. You can set a stop loss at $105 to lock in your previously unrealized profits from this trade.

Effectively, you sell your position automatically once this level has been reached, which allows you to not have to monitor charts 24/7. This helps you in cases where a stock falls rapidly and prevents you from facing huge losses in open positions. The one drawback of relying solely on stop loss orders is that, if the volume is not there at your stop loss price, and the price continues to fall, your order will not execute and your position will still be open.

You can also use stop losses when shorting coins to prevent losses if the price increases after you place your short-sale.

A stop limit order is slightly different because you set both the maximum and minimum level you are willing to buy a particular coin. Let's say you want to buy Bitcoin at $95, but it is currently trading at $100, you can set a limit order so you automatically buy once it hits $95. But you can also set the order to automatically sell at $120 if it reaches that level. By doing this, you can step away from the computer, and providing the stock reaches those levels, the trade will execute automatically.

What you should set your stop loss at depends on your risk persona. Traditional trading advice recommends a 2% stop loss for each order, however with cryptocurrency's volatility, this may well be too conservative a measure and will result in excessive losses. I advise you to experiment for yourself and decide on your own personal stop loss point.

Note: For both stop loss and stop limit orders, you can employ a strategy of placing many smaller stop losses, which total up to your position in the coin - this prevents issues like a lack of volume to fulfill them. This isn't always necessary, but it worth doing as a precautionary step.

Margin Trading

Disclaimer: Margin trading is extremely risky, only do this if you can afford to lose everything you invest. Never ever short on margin in the cryptocurrency market.

If you're unaware of what margin trading is, Investopedia sums it up with this analogy

"Imagine this: you're sitting at the blackjack table and the dealer throws you an ace. You'd love to increase your bet, but you're a little short on cash. Luckily, your friend offers to spot you $50 and says you can pay him back later. Tempting, isn't it? If the cards are dealt right, you can win big and pay your buddy back his $50 with profits to spare. But what if you lose? Not only will you be down your original bet, but you'll still owe your friend $50. Borrowing money at the casino is like gambling on steroids: the stakes are high and your

potential for profit is dramatically increased. Conversely, your risk is also increased."

Many cryptocurrency exchanges allow you to trade on margin, which is essentially borrowing money from the exchange in order to trade. Bitfinex allows for 3.3:1 margin trading, so for every $1 you have in your trading account, you can trade up to $3.3 on margin in the cryptocurrency markets. This is by no means the largest margin offered either, Kraken for example allows for 5X leverage on Bitcoin. BitMex, another exchange, allows for 100X margin, meaning you can literally borrow $100 for every $1 of your own money.

The reason exchanges allow margin trading is because the overall trade volume is higher, and therefore their fees are higher as well.

As a new trader, you should never trade using leverage. You are too inexperienced to be able to handle the potential losses that margin trading brings. Drops of 20 or 30% are not uncommon in crypto markets, and those drops are magnified when you are margin trading and can potentially wipe out your entire trading account.

Trading on margin also makes you vulnerable to flash crashes, such as in June 2017 when Ethereum fell from $360 to $13 for a brief period on GDax. Anyone trading on margin would have seen their funds wiped out in an instant.

Cryptocurrency Trading Bots

If you're not familiar with trading bots, they are automated pieces of software that perform technical analysis on stock, bonds or in these case, cryptocurrency. Ever since the boom in online trading, these bots have been synonymous with scams, pyramid schemes and other guaranteed money losers for those who use them.

The cryptocurrency world is no different, and I can safely say that the majority of trading bots on the market today are either completely useless or an outright scam.

Bonus Mistake 10.5: Believing "too good to be true" trading software or services

Cryptocurrency Bot & Trading Software Scams

CryptoRobot365

After defrauding hundreds of users, and receiving countless negative testimonials from those who never recovered their money, it's safe to say CryptoRobot365 should be well and truly avoided. To make matters worse, not only will you lose money, but your personal information may also be at risk.

The first warning sign is that this bot isn't registered with any regulated brokerages. The second being that although the software is advertised as free on signup, the actual minimum amount needed to have any access to the trading bot is a deposit of $250. The third sign being a fake "Best 2016 Performance Robot" icon on their website, when the site has only been registered since July 2017. The final nail in the coffin is that their testimonial page features a ton of fictitious testimonials using fake pictures and identities.

Unfortunately, as of the time of writing, the site still runs Google ads under popular keywords including "cryptocurrency trading bot". If you see it listed during a Google search, stay well away.

CryptoTrader.co

CryptoTrader.co's website opens with a man named Dave Richmond informing us that he can help us make $5,000 per day with his revolutionary new trading software. The software is apparently so good that he's turned 43 people into a millionaire last year! Notice any warning signs yet? Me too.

Like the above website, CryptoTrader.co also suffers from misinformation regarding how long the site has been functioning. The claims of making 43 people millionaire last year don't exactly hold up when the site has only been online for a few short months. The site also has no brokerage license or legal authority of any kind.

So with zero reviews on any independent websites, a website filled with a whole bunch of lies. An a frontman who appears to be a paid actor, CryptoTrader.co is definitely a no go as far as trading software websites.

Any person who approaches you with a trading bot

Occasionally if you hang out in enough cryptocurrency trading groups on social media or Telegram, someone will message me saying they have this great bot for sale at a surprisingly low price. If it looks too good to be true, it probably is. So stay well away from these low level scammers.

The only trading bot I recommend

HaasBot (http://bit.ly/HaasSatoshi) by HaasOnline is the only auto trading platform I recommend using. In a sea of scams and dodgy platforms, its nice to see a group with an ethical foundation.

The reasons for this recommendation are as follows: First of all, they refer to the operation as a trading platform rather than a trading bot. What they are actually selling is a software that numerous bots can be used with.

HaasOnline is completely upfront about what their bots *can* and more importantly *cannot* do. They don't make any vague guarantee about always beating the market like other bot or trading automation software does. Most importantly, they don't make any guarantees about monetary returns.

The software uses transparent technical analysis methods to perform trades. The bot uses this analysis to trade 24/7, and will add small amounts of volume needed to execute trades. There are also a number of safety features built in, to protect your investments.

Currently the bot supports over 500 different cryptocurrency pairings. Plus it is compatible with major cryptocurrency exchanges including Bitfinex, BitTrex and Poloniex. Where it may shine the most is with its built in arbitrage bot, which takes profits from the small difference between various pairings.

The team behind HaasOnline are based in the Netherlands, and there is a public figurehead in founder Stephen de Haas. In a discussion on popular Bitcoin forum bitcointalk.org, de Haas answered the questions "Can I get rich with this software?" in a frank manner.

"It's possible, but I can not guarantee this. As i stated before with speculation there is a risk involved. The main power of this simple trade bot is that it operated 24-hours a day. Meaning the bot will work for you when you are sleeping or working. This gives you the advantage of making more trades and possibly result in much higher profits."

Quality does come at a cost however, with the cheapest option being 0.09BTC (roughly $1000 at the time of writing), and the most expensive option being priced at 0.24BTC. However, this investment could be deemed as worth it by those looking to trade serious cryptocurrency volume, but can't dedicate 12+ hours a day to studying charts. The team also offers full, limited time refunds to those who use the software but for whatever reason do not like it.

Open Source Trading Software

There are a few open source platforms where developers have created their own trading bots for users to try free of charge. The two most popular of these are Gekko and ZenBot. Neither of these make any guarantees of profits, and were made more for experimentation than anything else. However as they are open source, and can be scrutinized by anyone, I'd thought I'd include them for those looking for a cheaper automated solution to their trading needs.

Trading Suicide

The following are moves that traders make that I consider trading suicide. Making any one, or more of these moves is generally a terrible idea, and **will lose you money** in the long run.

1. Adding to a clear losing position

Don't throw good money after bad. Let's say you've bought ETH at 300, and it's dropped to 270, but you're convinced it's going to rebound, do not top up your position. You may believe that by buying more at 270, your entry price averages out to 285, but you are unlikely to get back to this price before the stock drops even further. If you are clearly in a losing trade, close your position, get out, and live to trade another day.

2. **Focusing on single trades compared to long term profits**

Don't get attached to trades, especially bad ones. You may have thought you've done everything correctly, but sometime the market just knows better. Once again, get out, reset and live to trade another day.

3. **Checking prices of a coin after you've closed your position**

This is a subtle, yet deadly trading mistake that many losing traders make. It happens all too often, and leads to greed setting in for subsequent trades. Say you bought XMR at 180, and sold for 200, but you then see the price has gone up again to 215, and you start kicking yourself thinking "if only I'd held on a little bit longer", and you beat yourself up over your lost hypothetical profits.

The effect this has on your next trades is that it will cause you to hold onto positions for too long before closing, which inevitably leads to losses.

4. Chasing a coin past your initial target entry price

This is even more important if you're doing short term or day trading. You have a target entry price for a reason, because the charts say so. If for whatever reason you miss the entry price, then focus on another trade because your chances for profit has been drastically reduced.

5. Being impatient with winning trades, and being too patient with losing ones

Sometimes trades take time to play out, sufficient buyer demand may take a few days or even a week to appear, but as long as the price is moving sideways, you can keep the trade open. If you see downward movement however, it's best to get out as soon as possible and limit your losses.

6. Not deciding if you want more fiat, or more cryptocurrency

Cryptocurrency is unique in the respect that you can still make a good trade in terms of dollars, but you can lose money in terms of actual cryptocurrency gains. The best way to combat this, is to decide which cryptocurrency(ies) you want to make the most of, and focus on trading with that goal in mind, rather than flip flopping between USD gains and crypto gains.

7. Not having a target exit price when you enter a trade

This is a surefire way to lose money. You need to have a target exit price or profit % based on your technical analysis, otherwise you will end up chasing gains for too long, and inevitably lose money. On top of target exit price, you should have a rough idea of how long you want to stay in the trade for.

8. Trading in an unstable mood

This includes if you're under the influence of alcohol or narcotics. If you're in a bad mood, then don't trade. Your emotions will get the better of you, and you make stupid decisions and cost yourself money.

Conclusion

So there you have it. The biggest cryptocurrency trading mistakes that new traders make - and you can avoid them and become a profitable trader.

So remember, pick a trading strategy, and don't deviate from it.

Don't panic trade, and trade when you're in an unstable mood. Trade rationally, removing all emotion from the trade (as much as humanly possible anyway).

Only trade cryptocurrencies you're familiar with. So it's best to start with the ones with most liquidity like Bitcoin, Ethereum and Litecoin.

And trade on an exchange with low exchange fees, so your profits don't get eaten up the more you trade.

Utilize the spreadsheet I included to help you track your trades and identify patterns in your own trading.

I wish you the best of luck, and most importantly, I hope you make a lot of money with cryptocurrency.

Thanks,

Stephen

Resources:

The following are additional resources for everything from charting to trading psychology. Note, the majority of these are not cryptocurrency specific, nor am I affiliated with any of the authors.

Top 10 Trading Setups Explained by Ivaylo Ivanov - Focuses on traditional markets like stocks, but the lessons can be easily applied to cryptocurrency. The book shows you how to recognize overall market patterns and how to approach each one of them.

Technical Analysis of Stock Trends (9th Edition) by Robert Edwards and John Magee - If you're going to buy one "encyclopedia" of technical analysis, make it this one.

One Up on Wall Street by Peter Lynch - Lynch famously beat the market 15 years in a row. Much of his trading advice holds true today as much as it did when the book was first released. Note, the paperback version of this book is cheaper than the Kindle version for reasons unknown

Cryptocurrency: 13 More Coins to Watch with 10X Growth Potential in 2018

By Stephen Satoshi

Introduction - Cryptocurrency as we head into 2018

2017 was undoubtedly the year that Cryptocurrency arrived on the world stage. The total market cap surged from $18 billion on January 1st to over $600 billion by the end of the year. Coinbase became the world's number one most downloaded app and saw transaction volume increase by a factor of 30.

Bitcoin hit $20,000 per coin very briefly in December. Ethereum went from $9 to over $700, and Litecoin finally broke out and hit $300 by the end of the year. Average returns for investing over the 12 month period range from 200% on the low end, to over 1000%.

Frankly, if you put money into cryptocurrency in 2017, it was near impossible to lose.

One of the most startling statistics of 2017 was that if you had invested $100 into the top 10 market cap coins on January 1st, you would have seen returns of $43,000 over the course of the year.

But how does that affect us going forward? Will we have a repeat of last year and see gigantic market growth once more? We'd all sure like to hope so. It's likely though that the market will be a little more nuanced as we progress.

It's clear now that cryptocurrency isn't just "internet gimmick money", we are truly witnessing the birth of a brand new asset class. Institutional money is flowing into the market just as fast as consumer money. There are multiple cryptocurrency ETFs in the works and

December saw the launch of Bitcoin futures on CME, the world's largest futures exchange.

But to those of us who are in search of projects with potential for huge growth, 10X, 100X or even 1000X growth, that we now know is completely possible within the cryptocurrency space, we have to dig a little deeper. That's why in this book I'm listing 13 coins with huge possibilities in 2018. Coins with exciting ideas, projects and use cases. Some of them may be more familiar to you than others, but every single one of them has been hand picked based on my own criteria, and you can rest assured that many other coins were discarded in the selection process.

I wish you the very best in your cryptocurrency investing journey, and I hope you make a lot of money.

Thanks,

Stephen

Factors that affect coin growth

Continued Adoption

It's easy to forget sometimes that we are still very much in the early stages of the market. Cryptocurrency may have quickly reached a $600 billion market cap, but that is still dwarfed by the $200 trillion market cap of stocks, cash, gold and bonds combined. And blockchain technology as a whole still has a huge amount of growing to do.

Adoption of coins both as payment methods for currency based coins, as well as, partnerships with larger corporations for non-currency based ones will lead to continued growth going forward.

Coinbase

Coinbase, the cryptocurrency exchange app ended 2017 having hit the number one download spot on the Apple store and Google Play store. The vast majority of the new players into the market (and that may well include yourself), got their start with Coinbase. The convenience of being able to buy and sell cryptocurrency on the go using a credit card is something that favors mass adoption. Especially when compared to previous years when complex wire transfer processes made cryptocurrency much harder for the average person to buy.

As you may know, however, Coinbase currently only deals with 3 cryptocurrencies. Namely, Bitcoin, Ethereum and Litecoin. However, Coinbase Co-Founder and CEO Asiff Hiriji stated in December 2017 that the platform plans to add more coins in the coming months. With rumors about which coins would be added driving up the price of a number of altcoins including Ripple and Bitcoin Cash.

Needless to say, the next coin to be added on Coinbase will see short term positive effects regardless of its long term potential. Much of the cryptocurrency buying public won't be able to wait to get their hands on the shiniest new coin. However, exactly which coins would be added is still largely unknown, although we can make some educated guesses into which ones *won't* be next in line.

Monero - Its status as a complete privacy coin conflicts with Coinbase's position as an SEC regulated entity and their anti-money laundering provisions. The same applies to coins like **ZCash.**

Neo - NEO is not divisible like other cryptocurrencies, and could technically be classified as a security which pays a dividend (in the form of GAS). This makes it hard for Coinbase to add it due to being bound by SEC regulations.

It should also be noted that there are multiple fake images online showing Dash, Monero and Ripple added to Coinbase. Please check the official website before buying or selling on other exchanges based on news of Coinbase additions.

Update: As of December 20th 2017, Bitcoin Cash was added to Coinbase

Bitcoin

Like it or not, Bitcoin's price still carries a lot of the new money being flooded into the market. Although this may prove to be less of an issue going forward as many first time buyers are now investing in Ethereum or

Litecoin as their first venture into the cryptocurrency market, Bitcoin is still a major factor in determining overall market sentiment.

The cryptocurrency flowchart generally goes like this.

1. New investors buy Bitcoin with fiat currency as their first foray into the market > Bitcoin's price goes up
2. As Bitcoin's price goes up, altcoin holders move their money into Bitcoin > Altcoin prices go down
3. If Bitcoin's price falls, those holding Bitcoin cash out to fiat, signaling decreased market confidence > Bitcoin & altcoin prices go down
4. If Bitcoin's price remains stable, investors begin to look for new opportunities and begin researching and buying altcoins > altcoin prices rise

If you track the BTC vs. Altcoin patterns in 2017, this generally holds true. Altcoins perform best when Bitcoin prices are stable, and not moving much in either direction. Large movements in Bitcoin price generally have negative effect on altcoin prices.

Legislation

Cryptocurrency leglisation is still a hot topic, and one where we are still largely in the unknown. Poorly researched news articles with headlines such as “Chinese government bans Bitcoin” tend to be the ones that are the most read, even if their factual accuracy is debatable at best.

Cryptocurrency at its core ideals has always been a decentralized idea. In other words, the entire existence is predicated on moving away from control by a single central government. However, in practical terms, especially where investments and securities are concerned, there does have to be some form of recognition by governments, at a national level at least.

For US citizens, the number one short term concern would be senate bill including digital currencies as part of current anti-money laundering laws. These laws would force traders to reveal indentities in certain circumstances, which would obviously hamper the growth of privacy based cryptocurrencies such as Monero, ZCash and Verge. This is also a concern for both UK and EU citizens, whose governments are working on their own version of similar rulings.

Asian legislation is another area of concern, with China and South Korea being under the spotlight specifically. These two markets represent the largest portion of the cryptocurrency space, and government clampdowns from both of these countries have had negative effects on the overall market as recently as mid 2017.

Atomic Swaps

Atomic swaps are one of the most fascinating cryptocurrency developments as we move into 2018, and one that is sure to affect many coins going forward. Atomic swaps allow coin conversions, without the need for a third party. For example, if you own 1 Bitcoin and your friend owns 100 Litecoin, and you want to swap. Currently you would have to use a third party exchange to do so. Third party exchanges require both fees and a degree of trust.

However, by using atomic swaps, there is no need for a third party as both the sender and recipient could confirm the transaction themselves by using what is known as a hash-time limited contract (HTLC). An HTLC is essentially a one-time code that would be generated as part of the swap, that is required to verify its success. If the code is not entered by either party, the transaction will be reversed and both parties will receive their initial coins back.

Up to this point, we have only seen atomic swaps used in very limited amounts, because cryptocurrencies are running on different blockchains, and we need them to share the same cryptographic hash function. The implementation of Lightning Network would allow this to occur. Currently, successful atomic swaps have been carried out between Litecoin, Bitcoin, Vertcoin and a few other coins. Coins that are capable of atomic swaps may well have significant first mover advantage going forward.

Coin Prices & Fractions

I know what you're thinking, I bought this book just to be told the price of a coin matters?! First, let me expand on this rather obvious statement. Cryptocurrencies are unique in the sense that many of them (with notable exceptions like Neo) are divisible into tiny fractions. Bitcoin, for example, is available down to 8 decimal digits, so you could go on an exchange and buy 0.0000001 Bitcoin.

Why does this matter? Simply put, it's extremely confusing to new investors who have previously only bought entire shares of companies. Therefore, they would rather buy 1 of a certain cryptocurrency, than a fraction of another - especially if there are no other deciding factors between the two. It appears easier to buy a "whole" of one coin versus a fraction of another. Therefore, coins with a low $ price are inherently more attractive, even if they have a huge market cap and have less room for potential growth than coins with a lower supply and market cap, but a high $ price per coin.

For example, Ripple currently trades at around $0.50 per XRP, and is seen as "cheap" by many inexperienced buyers, despite its huge market cap. The same applies to Stellar Lumens which trades at around $0.28 per XLM.

Factors to Consider Before Investing

While larger cryptocurrencies like Bitcoin, Ethereum and Litecoin have long track records and multiple real world functions, some of the coins mentioned in this book do not - hence their lower price.

There are a number of different variables to investigate before you undertake any investment, and cryptocurrency has its own set.

Proof of Concept (PoC)

In other words, does the technology have a working model, or is it still in a theoretical stage. Obviously more mature coins will have a higher value, with the more theoretical coins being a bigger risk. As the different coins here are in different stages of their life cycle, that is up for you to decide.

The Development Team

Who are the developers and what is their track record? Particularly within the cryptocurrency and blockchain space. Another thing to consider their record within the particular industry they are targeting, and if they have industry connections are not.

The Utility Of The Coin

Ideas are great, but if the coin token itself doesn't have usage, then the true potential of the project must be questioned. This is especially true in the case of certain coins where the theory and market potential checks out, but the question of "why can I just use Bitcoin/Litecoin to do the same thing" is often raised.

The Roadmap

Roadmaps are important for short-term gains because they set out development targets for the coin. If these goals are reached and the products/platforms move from alpha to beta to a fully launched product, then that only means positive things for the coin and its value. However continually missed targets are a red flag.

Which exchanges is the coin listed on

Many of these coins are still only available on smaller exchanges. Once the coin is listed on larger exchanges, with Coinbase being the biggest and most accessible, the coin has greater visibility and this leads to a rise in value.

Mining Algorithm - Proof of Work vs. Proof of Stake vs. Proof of Signature

You'll notice later on when discussing individual coins that I talk about which mining algorithms are used. The two most popular are Proof of Work (PoW), used by Bitcoin and Proof of Stake (PoS), which will be used by Ethereum from Q4 2017 and beyond, and is currently used by a number of Ethereum based tokens. There is also Proof of Signature (PoSIGN), which is used by newer projects including Xtrabytes.

How to Buy Bitcoin, Ethereum or Litecoin

Gone are the days when buying cryptocurrency was a time consuming and somewhat uncomfortable endeavor. Nowadays buying Bitcoin and other popular cryptocurrencies is a similar process to exchanging currency when you go on vacation.

If you haven't purchased any cryptocurrency before, what you need to do first is to use fiat currency (USD, EUR, GBP etc.) to purchase cryptocurrency via an exchange. These exchanges function the same way as regular foreign currency exchanges do. The prices fluctuate on a daily basis, and like regular currency exchange markets - they are open 24/7. Exchanges make their money by charging a small fee for each transaction.

Some charge both buyers and sellers, some only charge a fee for buying. For security reasons, most of these exchanges will require you to verify your ID before allowing you to purchase cryptocurrency.

It is also important to note the type of payments each exchange supports. Some allow for debit/credit card payments whereas other only accept PayPal or bank wire transfers.

Coinbase

Currently largest currency exchange in the world, Coinbase allows users to buy, sell and store cryptocurrency. Coinbase is undoubtedly the most beginner friendly exchange for anyone looking to get involved in the cryptocurrency market. They currently allow trading of Bitcoin, as well as, Ethereum and

LiteCoin using fiat currency as a base. Known for their stellar security procedures and insurance policies regarding stored currency. The exchange also has a fully functioning iPhone and Android app for buying and selling on the go, very useful if you are looking to trade.

Once you are signed up and complete the identity verification procedures you can buy Bitcoin with your credit or debit card instantly.

Coinbase also recently launched the Coinbase Vault, which is a secure way of storing your cryptocurrency while still having it accessible to trade. The vault uses double email address + phone verification in order to access your funds. If you're planning on holding long-term, I still recommend offline storage - but as an intermediary option, the Vault is a step in the right direction.

If you sign up for Coinbase using this link, you will receive $10 worth of free Bitcoin after your first purchase of more than $100 worth of cryptocurrency.

http://bit.ly/10dollarbtc

Note: As of 12/20/17 - Coinbase now also allows users to buy and sell Bitcoin Cash

How do I buy these altcoins if I can not buy them in my local currency?

Buying altcoins can be confusing at first because the vast majority of them aren't available to buy in exchange for fiat currency. Therefore, there are a few steps to go through, but not to worry, because here is a step by step guide to buy altcoins.

1. **Create an account on Coinbase**

Coinbase is still the easiest way for most people to get involved in the cryptocurrency market. Once you sign up (remember to use the link http://bit.ly/10dollarbtc

to get $10 worth of Bitcoin for free after your first transaction)

2. **Buy Bitcoin, Ethereum or Litecoin**

You can either do this directly on Coinbase, or by transferring your money to Coinbase's sister site GDax which has lower transaction fees. You can use your Coinbase login credentials to access GDax.

Once you have bought your coins, they will be automatically transferred to your wallet on the respective site. Remember, if you are buying purely for the sake of exchanging coins for the altcoins mentioned in this book, then I recommend buying ETH rather than BTC because the transfer fees will be much lower.

3. **Send coins to your exchange of choice**

I have listed which exchanges to buy these coins at, on the individual coin page under "where to buy". Create an account on that particular website and go to the "deposit" page. Once on the page select your respective coin's wallet (double check you haven't selected the wrong one), and generate an address

You address will be a string of alphanumeric characters similar to this 0x0ded6e1e425eeb3876269c6ae93df77944acf4eee4fe1d7ccd77b185dce1d207

Go to the send coins page on your Coinbase/GDax account and copy the above address into the "recipient" box, and click confirm. This will show your transaction fee as well (for ETH it is currently around $0.40 per transaction).

4. **Use your coins to exchange for altcoins**

Once the transaction has gone through and your coins are now showing up in your new wallet, you can exchange them for the altcoins of your choice. For example, if you want to buy XLM, you can select the XLM/ETH pairing on the exchange.

How to save up to $20 on each altcoin transaction

One of the major problems we face right now in cryptocurrency is the sheer strain on the network as it tries to keep up with increased demand. Transaction fees and transaction times have been dramatically increasing since Mid-November, and new investors are realizing the hard way when they try to transfer their coins from where they bought them, to another exchange.

Many websites give instructions of "Buy bitcoin first, then send to an exchange". However, this is fundamentally wrong and will cost you money. It is much cheaper to buy and send Ethereum for the purpose of exchanging it with one of the coins listed below. The same applies to Litecoin, but there are much fewer Litecoin/altcoin pairs available when compared to Bitcoin and Ethereum.

Currently the approximate transaction prices for each coin are as follows

Bitcoin: $17

Ethereum: $0.40

Litecoin: $0.13

Coins to Watch in 2018

WaBi (WABI)

Price at Time of Writing: $2.00

Market Cap at Time of Writing: $90,339,960

Available on:

BTC: Binance

ETH: Binance, EtherDelta

Where to store:

WaBi can be stored on MyEtherWallet or the Mist desktop wallet

WaBi is a Chinese based blockchain initiative that focuses on anti-counterfeiting for physical products. Born out of the 2012 Chinese milk scandal, that saw 6 children die and over 50,000 hospitalized as a result of fake baby milk formula, the project aims to battle the $500 billion counterfeiting industry.

WaBi's solution to this is linking products using RFID labels with a built-in anti-counterfeit measure. Using Walimai's anti-counterfeiting RFID technology allows consumers to verify the authenticity of the product using their smartphone. Blockchain technology comes into this by verifying product authenticity on a decentralized digital ledger that would allow anyone to see which products are authentic and which ones are not. This essentially creates a secure link between the digital and physical domains. This has ramifications for so many consumer goods industries including baby food, pharmaceuticals, alcohol, clothing and electronics.

This bold venture faces many challenges, especially as there are physical products involved, which in itself has its own set of hurdles. For example, deterioration of product labels, can the labels be securely attached for the entirety of the product's lifespan, and if not, can they be replaced with counterfeit labels?

However, after 3 years of development, the WaBi team has now successfully created a working product as of December 2016, and their tags feature both a unique encrypted product ID and geolocation data of the product source I.e. which factory it was manufactured at. So counterfeiters would have to be able to replicate both of these if they wanted to produce a fake version of the same product, which would prove near impossible unless they have access to the exact same factory where the authentic version of the product is produced.

There is also the issue of consumer trust, can consumers really be sure that the authenticity data is accurate? Well, that's where blockchain technology comes in. Because records are publicly available, and constantly updated in real time, there is no inherent reason not to trust them.

The next level of this trust is the facilitation of consumer to consumer or peer to peer sales. The problem with traditional peer to peer platforms like eBay, and newer ones such as social media based selling, has always been the prevalence of counterfeit goods. As this selling platforms are not under the same legal scrutiny as traditional ones, sellers of counterfeit goods often get away with it. By utilizing WaBi technology, a potential buyer can verify the authenticity of any product *before* the sale goes through, which ensures that all transaction and products are legitimate. The platform has already undergone testing in China, both in ecommerce and in physical stores.

The WaBi token itself will be given to customers every time they scan an item. There are plans for these token to then be used as a loyalty incentive for customers to purchase products with the token as opposed to cash.

2018 will see WaBi roll out to over 1,000 stores across China. Price action in the short term will largely dependent on the token being available on more exchanges because Binance alone is not enough to support increased token demand.

Neo (NEO)

Price at Time of Writing - $72.25

Market Cap at Time of Writing - $4,696,120,000

Available on:

Fiat: Yunbi (CN), Jubi (CN), Livecoin

BTC: Bittrex, Binance, Bitfinex

ETH: Bittrex

Where to store:

Wallets are available on the official Neo website

I previously discussed Neo in my first book *Cryptocurrency: Beginners Bible.* Since then the price has risen by over 900%, and a number of exciting new developments have occurred with the Neo project, so I thought an update would be appropriate as we move into 2018.

One of these earliest Chinese based blockchain projects, Neo, formerly known as Antshares prides itself on being open source and community driven. The coin has been compared to Ethereum in the sense that it runs smart contracts instead of acting as a simple token like Bitcoin. The project is developed by a Shanghai based company called ONCHAIN.

In a June 2017 press conference held at the Microsoft China HQ in Beijing, the Antshares founder Da Hongfei announced the rebranding to Neo as well as discussing other projects in the pipeline. These included collaborating with certificate authorities in China to map real-world assets using smart contracts.

Neo's base in China allows it unique access to the world's 2nd largest market and the largest cryptocurrency market. This of course is seen as a unique plus when compared to other cryptocurrencies. However current drawbacks include a limited number of wallets for the coin itself, and a lack of ICOs completed on the platform. As of December 2017, there has still only been 1 Neo ICO in the form of Red Pulse.

At the Microsoft China event - Srikanth Raju, GM, Developer Experience & Evangelism and Chief Evangelist, Greater China Region, Microsoft, said that ONCHAIN is "one of the top 50 startup companies in China." Support and positive press from a global powerhouse like Microsoft can only be a positive for Neo going forward.

Perhaps the biggest determining factor for NEO going forward is support from the Chinese government.

While other cryptocurrencies suffer from legal battles with governments, Neo's relationship with the leadership has been low key if somewhat positive, with founder Da Hongfei attending government conferences and seminars on cryptocurrency and blockchain technology. After China banned Chinese citizens from participating in ICOs in July 2017, the entire cryptocurrency market took a hit. Neo has the potential to change this. For example, a future ruling that ICOs built on Neo are legal in China would likely see Neo's popularity increase on a worldwide scale.

One thing to be wary of with Neo is once again, a Chinese factor. This time it's the language barrier, as much of the news about the coin is published in Chinese originally, there is significant potential for mistranslations in the English speaking world. For example, "partnerships" with Microsoft and Alibaba (China's largest eCommerce company) have been overstated due to poor translations from Chinese news sources. That doesn't mean collaborations like this aren't possible in the future, but you should always be wary of news coming out of China, especially where unofficial translations are involved.

In the commonly held Neo versus Ethereum debate, there is no reason why one coin has to "win" against the other. Blockchain technology increases in popularity year by year, and there is no reason that both projects cannot coexist. In the short-term at least I would expect DApps to be built on both platforms.

The smart contracts running on Neo include equities, creditor claims, bills and currencies. This also includes the ability to issue what is known as "digital identities", this is paramount if things like financial assets need to be registered on the platform, because it acts a failsafe and holds people accountable if they break the terms of agreements they have set up. These identities will use internationally agreed upon standards, and as such will be compliant in the eyes of regulators. This may contradict many people's idea of completely private blockchain transactions, where identities of all parties are anonymous, but total privacy is not needed for *all* blockchain projects.

Neo has a number of developments planned for 2018, including NEOX, which will be Neo's version of atomic swaps and allow users to swap cryptocurrencies seamlessly without the need for an exchange. As of December 2017 though, this is still very much in the testing stage and the Neo team have not yet completed an atomic swap using NEOX. There are also several more ICOs planned for the platform.

It should also be noted for investing reasons, that one unique aspect of Neo, is that unlike most other cryptocurrencies, the coins are not divisible, so the smallest unit you can buy is indeed 1 Neo.

Gas (GAS)

Price at Time of Writing: $26.97

Market Cap at Time of Writing: $231,878,704

Available on:

Fiat: Coinnest (KOR)

BTC: Binance, Poloniex, OKEx

ETH: Poloniex

Where to store:

Note: Some exchanges will note credit your Gas if you hold Neo in their wallet. Binance definitely *does* credit it, but to make sure you should hold Neo in a non-exchange wallet.

If you've heard of Neo (or if you bought my first book back in August when it was trading at ~$7 as Antshares), then you've probably heard of Gas (previously Antcoins).

Gas is the token used to pay for transactions and service fees using the Neo network. So anytime someone sets up a smart contract, then Gas will be used as a means of payment for the network. It should be noted that the network is currently free as a means of garnering adoption in early stages, but this won't always be the case.

Essentially, Gas is the utility of the entire Neo ecosystem. Gas is what powers the Neo blockchain and allows the DApps built on it to function. Neo tokens on the other hand function more like shares in Neo as a whole.

You can earn Gas just by holding Neo in a wallet (so not on an exchange), currently if you hold 1 NEO, it would take approximately 22 years to generate 1 Gas. However, it may well be more profitable just to buy Gas itself. The thinking behind is the based on the Gas:Neo price ratio, which tends to hover between 0.3 to 0.5. However, many analysts believe the long term ratio will actually be closer to 0.8. This makes Gas an interesting play for higher potential gains than Neo itself. Especially as more and more DApps are launched on the Neo network, and these DApps require more Gas to function.

Right now the schedule of Gas produced by the Neo network is scheduled to end after 22 years (when all 100 million Gas tokens will be in circulation.) There is a caveat however as the Neo developers still reserve the right to produce more Gas tokens if necessary. The team also reserve the right to adjust the amount of

Gas required to use the network, however, this should not impact the price of Gas in theory (as they can simply divide the required price into fractions).

Right now the main issues with Gas prices have been that it is not as widely available on exchanges as Neo. For many months Gas was only available to buy on Chinese exchanges, and even at the time of writing, it only available on Binance and Poloniex. So let's make this entirely clear, due to the laws of supply and demand - **it is completely possible for Gas to be worth more than Neo in the short term.**

Stellar Lumens (XLM)

Price at Time of Writing: $0.28

Market Cap at Time of Writing: $5,064,226,845

Available on:

BTC: Bittrex, Binance, Kraken

ETH: Bittrex, Binance

Where to store:

A full selection of wallets including mobile, desktop and web-based are available on https://www.stellar.org/lumens/wallets/

XLM tokens are also compatible with the Ledger Nano S hardware wallet.

A late bloomer that saw some big price rises at the very end of 2017. Stellar Lumens is an intriguing project with a rather interesting history behind it.

Drawing obvious comparisons to Ripple, the Stellar network is focused on payment processing between large corporations and in the consumer to consumer space. The main difference however is that Stellar operates as a nonprofit organization that doesn't charge for use of the network. The initial funding for the project was from payment processor Stripe.

For example, you are an American who wants to send money to your friend who lives in Germany. Currently, you would have to pay large transaction fees to send Euros from your US bank. However, by using XLM (or

Lumens, the currency of the Stellar network). You could send USD, and your friend could withdraw money in Euros, without having to pay huge currency conversion fees. The current base fee for a transaction is just 0.00001 XLM, which is just a fraction of a penny, which is paid for by the sender. Like other blockchain projects, transactions on the Stellar network are publicly available and verifiable to prevent fraud occurring.

The Stellar team also focus on social causes, such as making saw a banking system is available to those who don't currently have access to one. The reduced fees, especially for those who need to frequently send money overseas, is a big selling point in the third world countries this initiative is targeting.

2017 was a big year for the Stellar project, Forbes magazine dubbed it "Venmo, but on a global scale - and for larger bodies like banks and corporations." The coin was added to larger exchanges like Binance and is now compatible with well known hardware wallet including the Ledger Nano S.

In October, the team announced a formal partnership with IBM and KickEx to “develop a blockchain-based cross-border payments solution proven to significantly reduce transaction costs and increase transaction speeds." This announcement kick started a price surge for Stellar which continued for the remainder of the year.

Stellar’s history is one that should be mentioned as well. It was founder in 2014 by Jeb McCaleb and Joyce Kim. McCaleb has history in the cryptocurrency space and was one of the founders of the Mt. Gox exchange, which at its peak was the largest cryptocurrency exchange in the world. McCaleb sold the exchange in 2011, shortly before the hacking incident that would result in Mt. Gox’s bankruptcy.

McCaleb then moved on to Ripple, but was made to leave the team after the Mt. Gox incident which deterred major financial institutions from wanting to deal with the project. This is where it gets dicey, after being asked, McCaleb announced that he would be liquidating his 9 billion XRP that he accumulated for his part in the project. He proceeded to do so in one lump sum and resulted in XRP's price crashing. He was then taken to court by Ripple and ended up losing the case.

This doesn't necessarily mean anything for Stellar going forward, and the project has been free of any controversy thus far. However I do feel it is important to take a look at the backgrounds of prominent team members, especially those with a track record like McCaleb's.

Moving into 2018, the success of Stellar Lumens will largely depend on the continued adoption of the platform. Partnerships with groups such as SatoshiPay, a web payment system that helps online publishers monetize their content is one such initiative. As of December 2017, the network was processing roughly 30,000 transactions per day with an average transaction time of 4 seconds.

The network does have built-in inflation to deal with the increasing volume of transactions. Currently, this rate is set at 1% per year. 5% of all Lumens (5 billion) are reserved for operating the network.

Groestlcoin (GRS)

Price at Time of Writing: $2.14

Market Cap at Time of Writing: $147,727,132

Available on:

Fiat: Litebit.EU (EUR)

BTC: Bittrex, Cryptopia, Livecoin

ETH: CoinExchange

LTC: Cryptopia

Where to store:

Wallets are available from

https://www.groestlcoin.org/downloads/

The rather strangely named Groestlcoin (pronounced "Grow-es-tul coin"), based off an Austrian word meaning quality and rigor, the coin has drawn comparisons to both Litecoin and Vertcoin. GRS is actually a pioneer in cryptocurrency in that it was the first coin to successfully utilize SEGWIT activation back in January 2017.

One of the key components of GRS is how easy it is to mine. If you've read any of my previous books, you'll know that I'm generally against at-home, consumer level mining for larger coins like Bitcoin and Ethereum, due high startup costs, electricity wastage and decreasing ROI year on year. However, GRS has seemingly found a workaround to this issue with their unique mining algorithm.

In their own words "You can mine with your old laptop and still turn over a profit", and power costs are far lower than mining larger coins, and the computer hardware needed is nowhere near as expensive.

In terms of actual use cases, GRS will function mainly for peer-to-peer transactions like Litecoin. There is also a privacy element (similar to Monero), by using the official Samurai wallet, users can use completely anonymous addresses with 256 bit encryption.

The coin also has a large number of available wallets (which many larger coins are still struggling with), including ones for less popular platforms like Blackberry and Linux. There are also plans to get hardware wallet support in early 2018.

One of the main determinants of the GRS price going forward will be the popularity of atomic swaps. This is a function where users can do coin-to-coin swaps for minimal transaction fees. Uptake of atomic swaps would allow users to exchange coins without having to rely on a centralized exchange.

Funnily enough, one of the sticking points in the GRS community is the name itself. There is a planned rebranding vote, with G2Coin being the most popular alternative suggestion right now. However, as of the time of writing, Groestlcoin remains the name, and GRS the symbol on exchanges.

Ultimately the success of GRS is in much the vein as the other "payment coins" such as Litecoin and Vertcoin. Can their features prove enough to reach wider adoption, especially in the face of mounting Bitcoin dominance in the space, which only appears to be getting stronger. After all, getting merchants or ecommerce stores to accept one crypto payment is one thing, but adopting 4 or 5 at once is whole other story. That being said, GRS is certainly one to watch based on the atomic swap factor alone.

Substratum (SUB)

Price at Time of Writing: $0.56

Market Cap at Time of Writing: $128,717,705

Available on:

BTC: Binance, HitBTC, KuCoin

ETH: Binance, HitBTC, EtherDelta

Where to store:

Substratum is an ERC20 token and can be stored using MyEtherWallet

Substratum is a blockchain project that focuses on the reallocation of unused computer resources. This has many applications such as web hosting and providing storage space for databases. Substratum aims to target both the institutional and consumer markets.

The main difference between this project and traditional cloud hosting services like Amazon Web Services or Rackspace, is that rather than paying for total uptime, users would pay per click on their site. So if you decide to host an unpopular website that doesn't get my traction, you won't be spending excess money on hosting that you don't need.

The platform also promises to be censorship free, so there would be no external monitoring or geo-restrictions in place. This is especially important in the times of net neutrality, where governments give internet service providers that right to charge more to access certain content.

The leads to the question of dealing with content that is deemed morally or legally bad such as terrorism or child pornography. As the network is decentralized, no single person or group has the ability to restrict what can or cannot be seen. Substratum users can vote to remove content from the network if it is deemed obscene or illegal. This voting system would be weighted so that it cannot be manipulated for personal gain by certain groups.

This is the area of the project that has come under the most scrutiny so far. Is a simple voting system enough or keep illegal content from being hosted? Following on, is there a potential workaround to this that doesn't involve a centralized body being in charge of what can and cannot be hosted on the network. Without a doubt, this is the biggest challenge the Substratum project faces in the short term.

Hosting on Substratum can be done by anyone with an internet connection, and hosts would be paid per click as well. The plans are for hosts to be able to run their service or “nodes” in the background without any disruption to their computer’s performance. These nodes would be dynamic, so if you are not using your computer, it would allocate more resources to hosting, and vice versa.

For web users, they won’t know the difference, it’ll just be like viewing any other web page.

The SUB token (known as Substrates) can be used to pay for hosting on the network, but a unique element is that it is not locked into the Substratum ecosystem. By integrating with CryptoPay, users can convert any unused SUB, or SUB they earn from hosting, into different cryptocurrencies or fiat currency, directly through the Substratum website. This kind of dynamic payment system is useful when compared to other cryptocurrency projects that force you to be locked into their particularly token, with no way of converting it without going onto a third party exchange.

Going forward, there are plans to release a public beta version of the platform in Q1 2018, and it will be extremely interesting to see how this goes, especially when related to the points above about hosting dubious content. If it can find a way to effectively deal with this, then there is no doubt in my mind that this project has a lot of room to grow going forward.

Modum (MOD)

Price at Time of Writing: $2.26

Market Cap at Time of Writing: $41,207,269

Available on:

BTC: Binance, Mercatox, Kucoin

ETH: Binance, EtherDelta

Where to store:

Modum is an ERC20 token running on the Ethereum blockchain, therefore it can be stored in MyEtherWallet.

Based out of Switzerland, Modum is a blockchain project that focuses on the supply chain management sector. It aims to provide a monitoring solution for transactions involving physical goods. The first industry Modum is targeting in the Pharmaceutical industry, which spends an approximate $3 billion a year on supply chain monitoring. Modum believes their solution could reduce shipping costs within the industry by as much as 60%.

What Modum does is monitor environmental conditions in the transit of goods. As many pharmaceuticals need specific conditions in order for the product to maintain its use (such as being refrigerated during transportation), it is vital that these conditions are met, and if they are not, it is equally vital that one of the parties be held accountable.

By using smart contracts, Modum allows companies to do this passively. For example, company A is purchasing drug X, which will be shipped from company B's warehouse. Drug X needs to be kept under 4 degrees centigrade during transit to maintain usability. By using Modum smart contracts, company A can verify that the drug was indeed kept under this temperature during transit, and when it arrived at company A's headquarters, a notification will go out, and payment will automatically be released. All of this can be monitored on both desktop and smartphone applications, in addition to a full range of backend data analytics.

The pharmaceutical industry is a wonderful test case as it requires great deal of supply chain integrity, and features a large amount of automation. The industry also has some of the highest standards required for product safety and security, so it's definitely a case of starting at the deep end for the Modum team.

Modum's main challenge is finding adoption from companies who would rather use Modum's solution as opposed to building their own in-house blockchain. Large corporate entities including IBM and Microsoft, are both dedicating large amounts of money to blockchain solutions of their own. It is worth noting that Modum's aim isn't to compete which large scale logistics operators, but to partner up with them and potentially license Modum devices to these larger companies for a best of both worlds solution.

Modum has obviously drawn comparisons to other blockchain projects such as WaltonChain, WaBi and VeChain, however, this isn't necessarily a bad thing. Supply chain management may well be the first widespread use case of blockchain technology. Therefore it's more than possible that all of these coins can co-exist. Modum is the only one of these projects based in Europe, a continent that has a whopping $1.2 trillion pharmaceutical industry.

In the short term, Q1 2018 should see the release of the first of Modum's product line, and an official entry into the Swiss market. The Modum also plans to step up their marketing efforts, which have been relatively lacking thus far. In the longer term, a real time tracking device is currently scheduled for Q1 2019, making Modum a project with long term viability as opposed to just short term monetary gains. Beyond the next couple of years, there is no reason that Modum cannot branch out beyond the pharmaceutical industry into supply chain management for other industries such as clothing. In a world full of hype and talks of 10X price increases in 1 month, I personally like Modum as a long-term hold with actual industry disruption possibilities.

One more interesting thing to note is that although Modum raised approximately $13 million worth of BTC and ETH during their ICO, due to the recent market bull run, this value has actually doubled since. Seeing as the team confirmed in December 2017 that they didn't yet sell any of their BTC or ETH received in the ICO, they have a larger pot to play with going into 2018, which could well see an accelerated roadmap moving forward.

XtraBytes (XBY)

Price at Time of Writing: $0.15

Market Cap at Time of Writing: $65,083,510

Available on:

BTC: Cryptopia, YoBit, C-Cex

LTC: Cryptopia

Where to store:

XtraBytes can be stored in wallets downloaded from https://www.xtrabytes.global/#wallet

XtraBytes aims to provide a decentralized cryptocurrency without dependency on inefficient, centralized mining operations. The projects will do this by using a newly created mining algorithm known as ZOLT which uses a Proof of Signature (PoSIGN) consensus method, as opposed to Proof of Work or Proof of Stake. The project has gathered some steam within the past few months and was the subject of an article on respected cryptocurrency website cointelegraph.com titled “Has XTRABYTES Already Rendered The Top Cryptocurrencies Obsolete?”

While that may be an overstatement at this stage of its development, the project is certainly an interesting one with a huge vision. A network of instant transactions, that are scalable combined with decentralized applications (DApps) that you can program in any language is an appealing proposition.

One of the first apps planned for the XBY ecosystem is X-Change, a decentralized cryptocurrency exchange. This will allow users to trade directly on the blockchain itself, without having to register for a third party exchange. This prevents incidents such as a centralized server being hacked, and user funds being stolen, like was the case with Mt. Gox exchange back in 2014.

Another planned project is X-Vault, a decentralized data storage applications that would store user data in encrypted pieces or "shards" across the network. This would prevent anyone from being able to access user data because even if they could "hack" one part of the network, they would only be able to access a tiny portion of the data. There are also additional plans for a decentralized instant messaging service as well as a platform for designed and executing smart contracts.

Currently, the project has managed to perform over 1,000 transactions per second on the TestNet, with a theoretical maximum of over 10,000 transactions per second. For comparison, Ethereum currently does around 20 transactions per second, albeit on a larger scale. Visa currently handles around 1,800 transactions per second.

XtraBytes has a long way to go before it can compete with larger projects in a similar vein like Cardano and EOS. A successful launch of both X-Change and X-Vault, even in beta form is likely to have positive price action as we move forward. A concentrated marketing effort is also needed if the coin is to receive more traction. It is important to note that much XBY's technology is still either in testing or theoretical stage, which explains its lower price and marketcap compared to some of the other projects mentioned here. However, a project with as much potential as this one should absolutely be on your radar in 2018 and beyond.

RaiBlocks (XRB)

Price at Time of Writing: $3.28

Market Cap at Time of Writing: $436,917,146

Available on:

BTC: BitGrail, Mercatox, BitFlip

Where to store:

Online wallets are available from

https://raiwallet.com/

Other desktop wallets are available on the official website https://raiblocks.net/

Currently hardware wallet support is planned for Q1 2018

RaiBlocks aims to use blockchain technology to facilitate peer-to-peer transactions in a fast, costless manner. RaiBlocks does this by using an unconventional blockchain variant known as a "block-lattice", in which easy user runs their own blockchain, known as an "account-chain", which allows for faster transactions. The ultimate goal is for XRB to become a fast, feeless way for a regular person to move their money around. This has led to XRB being dubbed "Blockchain 3.0" by some commentators.

Since each user runs their own account chain, both the sender and the recipient are required to confirm the transaction, unlike the traditional model which only requires confirmation from the sender. Although for convenience, the recipient of the transaction can confirm it at a later date, so it doesn't require them to be online at the time the transaction is sent.

One of the major advantages of this model is that transaction are infinitely scalable in theory because individual transactions settle regardless of other network activity. Therefore there is no "transaction queue", which we have seen with other cryptocurrencies, notably Bitcoin. This also means traditional mining algorithms like Proof of Work, are not necessary to verify the transaction.

Another major advantage of this model compared a traditional one, is the overall security of the network. In theory, one could take down the entire Bitcoin or Litecoin network without owning a single dollar worth of either currency. With XRB, you would need to own 51% of all the XRB in the world to coordinate such an attack, making it not only financially pointless but also a waste of time from a moral or ethical standpoint.

After all, why would you want to take down a network that you own the majority of?

RaiBlocks price going forward will largely be determined by the team's ability to get on major exchanges. With the majority of the volume currently traded on BitGrail, which is a relatively tiny exchange when compared to giants like Binance and Bittrex. Long time price determinants will be mass adoption, both on a peer-to-peer basis, and for a consumer-to-business payment system. The latter is something many coins are trying to achieve, and it is unlikely there is space for all of them going forward. It remains to be seen how much of that space XRB will take up, and as such, it should be viewed as a speculative investment.

In terms of competitor coins, IOTA is the obvious one, as their missions are largely the same, and neither of them requires any kind of mining or mining resources. However, RaiBlocks does have an advantage in that their network doesn't require Proof of Work to maintain security, and thus their long term costs are much lower. Another major difference is that XRB allows you to reuse addresses for transactions, an issue that IOTA faced when a few users lost a lot of currency because they tried to receive IOTA at an address they had already used. It should be noted that nearly every other cryptocurrency allows you to reuse a wallet address, so this is very much an IOTA problem rather than a cryptocurrency problem. There is an additional project in Radix, but it is still largely under development and far behind the other two at this stage.

Nav Coin (NAV)

Price at Time of Writing: $2.63

Market Cap at Time of Writing: $163,670,064

Available on:

Fiat: LiteBit.eu (EUR)

BTC: Bittrex, Poloniex, Cryptopia

LTC: Cryptopia

Where to store:

You can download wallets from https://navcoin.org/downloads/ - by using these wallets you can stake your coins and earn 5% interest on them

Based out of New Zealand and dubbed "The world's first fully anonymous cryptocurrency", Nav coin is one of the older projects around having started in 2014 as a fork of Bitcoin with greater optimization. For example Nav transaction times are around 30 seconds as opposed to Bitcoin's 10 minutes, as well as optional anonymous transactions. Nav also has low transactions fees, which currently amount to around $0.03 per transaction.

Nav's anonymity element is interesting because it uses a different anonymity algorithm to other major privacy coins. The two major algorithms in use are CryptoNote/Ring CT, which is used by Monero, and ZKSnarks, which is used by ZCash. These algorithms are both relatively new, and have little literature or regulated studies performed on their security, which is paramount for any network that claims to be anonymous.

Nav on the other hand uses the RSA algorithm, which is the most studied of the three. The RSA algorithm uses 2048 bit length keys, which are near impossible to hack via brute force.

Nav uses Proof of Stake (PoS), as opposed to Proof of Work (PoW). Not only is PoS a more environmentally friendly way of mining, as it doesn't require giant mining farms, it also allows you to earn interest on your coins by "staking" these coins to help run the network. PoS would also require any network attacker to own 51% of the coins themselves in order to coordinate an attack on the network.

Nav's big development move going forward is the release of NavPay and Polymorph. NavPay is a mobile wallet that would allow anonymous transactions between wallets, nothing too special there right? However, when combined with Polymorph, this would allow anonymous transactions of coins through coin transfer programs like Changelly. This is convenient because it allows cryptocurrency to cryptocurrency swaps without having to register for many different online exchanges. You can think of this like atomic swaps, but with an added privacy element. So for example, you could anonymously exchange your LTC to BTC, using Nav as the intermediary currency. So even if your base currencies do not have a privacy element, you could use Nav as the go-between to take advantage of a private transaction.

QASH (QASH)

Price at time of writing - $0.98

Market cap at time of writing - $346,077,200

Available on:

Fiat: Bitfinex, Quoine (USD & JPY)

BTC: Bitfinex, Quoine, Qryptos

ETH: Huobi, Qryptos

Where to store:

You can store QASH using MyEtherWallet by adding it as a custom token. Alternatively, you can store it on the Qryptos exchange in the short term.

QASH (also known as the Quoine Liquid Token) is one of the most interesting cryptocurrency projects as we head in 2018. The Quoine Liquid Platform plans to become the world's premiere cryptocurrency trading platform by combining liquidity from multiple markets.

Currently the global foreign exchange market for traded fiat currencies stands at around $5-6 trillion per day. Cryptocurrency's average trading volume is around $3 billion per day, but continues to grow on a monthly basis. The biggest problem the cryptocurrency market faces however is limited liquidity, especially when we are talking about the lesser known cryptocurrencies. Most cryptocurrencies are only liquid in a few pairings, and this varies from exchange to exchange. For example, there may be a lot of BTC/Neo liquidity on one exchange, but little on another. This also applies to many less used fiat to crypto pairings such as Canadian dollars, New Zealand dollars and Philippine Pesos. Citizens of these countries should all be able to access the cryptocurrency market, but they are currently being limited by lack of volume from their respective currency.

The Quoine Liquid platform plans to solve this problem by aggregating various liquidity sources into one single giant tradable order book. In other words, by combining liquidity from multiple markets, there is now enough to be able to fill everyone's orders. This would also allow buyers to buy cryptocurrency in their currency of choice, without having to convert to a more popular fiat currency first. The end result of this is that users would be able to effectively trade on any global exchange, without having to register or hold funds on that exchange.

QASH aims to become the world's first prime brokerage for cryptocurrency. This means they would offer a multitude of services including securities trading, credit facilities including lending, and leveraged trading. Prime brokerages appeal to institutional clients as well as to consumer clients.

Where the QASH token comes in is as a means of payment for using all services tied to the Quoine Liquid platform, such as transaction fees, as well as a token that is tradable on the open market like other cryptocurrencies. QASH holders will receive a 5% discount for transactions on the platform, with no maximum limit. This is especially important when we factor in prime brokerages into this, because a 5% discount on a transaction of $50,000,000 (not uncommon for prime brokerages), represents huge savings to the client.

QASH will initially be built on the Ethereum blockchain using ERC-20 tokens. Going forward, the team plans to migrate the project onto their own blockchain in mid 2019.

One of the major advantages of QASH is that the Liquid platform is already complete and online. At the time of writing the platform supports 15 different cryptocurrencies. The platform is fully licensed and regulated by the Japan Financial Services Agency.

The big growth factor for QASH and the Liquid Platform going forward will be adoption from institutional clients. If their first to market approach is successful, they could see an influx of large clients from Asia and beyond and this would provide them with a significant advantage of their competition. This alone makes QASH a cryptocurrency to watch as we move into 2018.

Cardano (ADA)

Price at time of writing - $0.50

Market cap at time of writing - $13,003,955,572

Available on:

Fiat: Coinnest (ROK)

BTC: Bittrex, Binance

ETH: Binance, Bittrex

Where to store:

You can store Cardano using their official Daedulus Wallet https://daedaluswallet.io/ - please note, at the time of writing there is an unofficial Daedulus Wallet listed on the Google Play Store. **For safety precautions do not download any Cardano wallets from the Google Play Store**

Cardano aims to become the world's most advanced open source smart contract platform. It can also boast of being the first ever cryptocurrency project that has been completed peer reviewed by a group of academic researchers. Cardano is built using the Haskell programming language, a language that is not often used in cryptocurrency projects, but one that can be considered one of the more secure, and least prone to errors.

Cardano can be seen as the 3rd generation of cryptocurrency, in that the project aims to revolutionize how we see blockchain technology as a whole by developing what the Cardano team believes is a fairer and more balanced ecosystem. This is opposed to first generation cryptocurrency like Bitcoin that merely function as a peer-to-peer monetary transaction system. On important distinction to make is that while other cryptocurrencies began as, and continue to be a work in progress, Cardano took the decisions to work on the project behind the scenes, and bringing to market a protocol that would be able to handle future adaptation.

The project uses a unique Proof of Stake (PoS) mining algorithm known as Ouroboros, as opposed to a Proof of Work algorithm.

An important element of the Cardano project is what they term the “social element of money”, in other words, how particular communities interact with their money. This makes sense if you think about the broader scale of different cryptocurrencies. For example, Bitcoin and Litecoin have very few technical differences between them, the same goes for Ethereum and Ethereum Classic. However, all 4 of these cryptocurrencies still maintain large communities supporting them and each of them have large market capitalizations.

Where Cardano comes in is the ability for users to propose changes in how their cryptocurrency of choice operates. This could be from voting on which projects the development team devotes funds to, to how different markets should be regulated. Cardano does this by utilizing a decentralized trust fund, which will be collected from transaction fees on the network. In theory, any user can request funds from the trust, and a ballot system would be used to decide whether the request is fulfilled or not. This would solve disputes such as soft or hard fork debates that have adversely affected both the Bitcoin and Ethereum communities.

One of the key elements of Cardano is a balance between the privacy of users on the platform and the needs of regulators such as government bodies.

Cardano is very much a long term project, and the roadmap signals that the full platform is not scheduled for release until early 2019. Investing in a project without a working product is a high risk move, and if you do choose to invest in Cardano, you should do your due diligence before allocating any of your portfolio towards it.

Bitcoin Cash (BCH/BCC)

Price at time of writing - $3,547.70

Market cap at time of writing - $59,829,341,444

Exchanges:

Fiat: Coinbase (as of 12/20/17), BitHumb (ROK), Coinone (ROK), Kraken

BTC: Bittrex, Bitfinex, Poloniex

Where to store:

There are numerous wallets available for all platforms on http://bitcoincash.org

Bitcoin Cash is also supported by both Trezor and Ledger Nano S hardware wallets.

I suppose we should probably talk about Bitcoin Cash. Especially for those of you who are new to the market and are wondering why on Earth there are now 2 Bitcoins on Coinbase (as of 12/20/17). I've already discussed Bitcoin Cash in my first book, *Cryptocurrency: Beginners Bible,* however as there have been a number of major developments since then, I felt it would have been a disservice not to provide an updated version of my summary.

Bitcoin Cash (BCH) emerged as the result of a split or "hard fork" in the Bitcoin technology on August 1st 2017. The end-goal of Bitcoin Cash is to function as a global currency, in the founder's words, to be what Bitcoin was supposed to have been in line with the original vision for Bitcoin outlined in the 2008 whitepaper.

If you held Bitcoin before August 1st (or to be technical, all Bitcoin holders as of block 478558), you will have been credited with an equal amount of Bitcoin Cash. Coinbase finally did this on 12/20/17, the same day that Bitcoin Cash was added. Your BCH will have been deposited directly into your wallet. It should be noted however that not all exchanges credited user accounts with BCH, so it's worth double checking yours.

The split occurred out of problems with Bitcoin's ability to process transactions at a high speed. For example, the Visa network processes around 1,700 transactions per second whereas Bitcoin averages around 7. As the network continues to grow, so do waiting times for transactions. BCC aims to run more transactions, as well as, providing lower transactions fees.

One of the major solutions to this issue is increasing the size of each block, so that more data can be processed at once. Bitcoin Cash increases the block size to 8MB, as opposed to the 1MB size of Bitcoin. This is in line with solving the problems of scalability that Bitcoin was facing previously. The technology itself worked in the short-term, with the first Bitcoin Cash block registering 7,000 transactions compared with Bitcoin's 2,500.

The success of failure of Bitcoin Cash will largely depend on Bitcoin's own adoption of the SegWit technology, and the ability to process transactions quicker to act truly as a currency - rather than a speculative asset. Detractors have also raised security concerns about Bitcoin Cash.

Bitcoin Cash has been widely adopted by many cryptocurrency exchanges. At the time of writing, there are only a few months worth of data available and thus, no one has been able to execute any long-term trends or technical analysis of BCH as a commodity. As further adoption continues, the price may well continue to rise.

Early price rises for Bitcoin Cash have been largely driven by demand from South Korea, with over 50% of the total trade volume being seen on South Korean exchanges.

There are also now two divided camps within the Bitcoin movement, with the original Bitcoin (or Bitcoin Core) on one side, and Bitcoin Cash on the other.

Miners have been quick to adopt the currency as well due to its higher mining ROI when compared to Bitcoin. The decrease in mining difficulty (leading to greater rewards for mining) will continue to see for miners move their resources from Bitcoin into Bitcoin Cash.

As we move into 2018, arguably the biggest debate in the cryptocurrency community will be whether Bitcoin and Bitcoin Cash can co-exist, or if one will win out against the other. Once it was added to Coinbase, Bitcoin Cash once again reached near all time highs in value compared to Bitcoin, but 2018 will be a big year in determining if BCH is here to stay.

Note: Depending on your exchange, Bitcoin Cash may use the symbol BCC or BCH - double check before executing a trade

How to Identify Market Manipulation

When investing in any cryptocurrency, it's important to be aware of market manipulation in the form of coordinated pump and dump schemes. This is more prevalent with lower volume cryptocurrencies where manipulation is easier to perform.

It doesn't take much digging to find the groups behind these, a few Google searches bring up various groups on Telegram, a Russian cloud-based instant messenger app that encrypts users identities. These groups aren't exactly subtle about their intentions with names such as Crypto4Pumps and PumpKing. These groups coordinate mass buys of low cap cryptocurrencies to artificially inflate the price, then sell their holding at a higher price once the general public become aware of it.

The reason these schemes can exist is the lack of regulation in the cryptocurrency market. These schemes used to be prevalent in the form of email blasts, during the penny stock market craze back in the mid 2000s, before many of the largest groups were shut down by regulators like the SEC.

The groups release buy signals to their users ahead of time, who then prepare funds, before being alerted to which cryptocurrency to buy. Previous coins that have been targets of these include MagiCoin, Gnosis and Ubiq. Once the initial buys happen, the group moves to other channels to "spread the word" of a great buying opportunity.

The initial buyers are now ready to dump their coins at a profit, which then tanks the price of the coin. Leaving those who bought late at a huge loss.

So how can you avoid these? Simply look at volumes on exchanges, and if you see a tiny market cap coin with a giant increase then stay well away. Price rises of 50% in under an hour are not uncommon with these sorts of schemes. Most major exchanges allow you to sort by price increase in the past hour, and it's a metric worth looking at. So don't chase anything purely because you see a quick price rise and hope to get in on the action, chances are you are already too late. Remember to do your own research before investing in a coin, and invest without emotion or the hope of instant riches.

One big cryptocurrency to avoid - why you should be wary of Bitconnect

Bitconnect, which trades as BCC on many exchanges, should be avoided in my opinion. I make careful choices never to go out of my way to specifically recommend coins worth buying, and this book is my personal opinion and not financial advice.

However, I will take a stance against any cryptocurrency project that I believe gives the space a bad name, and Bitconnect does just that. Currently ranked #20 on CoinMarketCap.com with a total market cap of $1.7 billion, the project is heavily promoted on social media. Bitconnect has a huge a number of red flags around the project and I've laid them out below.

Red Flag 1: Bitconnect is a Bitcoin lending system that promises enormous gains for those who put money into the platform. Their website promises returns of 1% *per day,* which anyone with any understanding of finance will tell you is impossible to uphold in the long term without completely breaking the world's economy.

Red Flag 2: Bitconnect claims their trading bots will continuously make money in order to fulfill these returns, regardless of overall market conditions. If they really did have a bot capable of doing this, why would they need investors? Surely that complicates things and adds unnecessary risk for them?

Red Flag 3: A capital "lock up" period of 299 days. So every investor *must* keep their initial investment in the Bitconnect program for 299 days before being allowed to cash out. That seems fishy as other managed funds do not require this or any other sort of "minimum investment period".

Red Flag 4: No public blockchain transactions that can verify their trading bots effectiveness. This is blockchain after all, so why can't we see how well the bot is doing? Their marketing video doesn't mention the bot very much, because they concentrate more on how rich everyone involved in the project is.

Red Flag 5: Bitconnect was originally registered in the UK, but the company was shut down because it never filed any accounts.

Red Flag 6: Prominent cryptocurrency figures including Ethereum Founder Vitalik Buterin, Litecoin founder Charlie Lee, and billionaire blockchain investor Michael Novogratz have dismissed the project as a "Ponzi scheme" and "most likely a scam."

Red Flag 7: This is the big one. Their referral system. Bitconnect operates a 7 layer referral bonus system. A system where you receive a % bonus from your referrals, and a smaller percentage from their referrals, and then an even smaller percentage from their referral's referrals. Do you see where this is going? Does the phrase "pyramid scheme" spring to mind?

As usual, I encourage you to do your own research on top of what you read in this book. I would be extremely vary of any program in cryptocurrency or otherwise, that promises guaranteed returns, and for that reason along with the others listed above, I strongly urge you to avoid Bitconnect.

Cryptocurrency Golden Rules for Safety & Security

So now you've bought your coins, here's a guide on how to safely store them, as well as some general best practices to employ with cryptocurrency.

1. Never give your private key to anyone

Your private key is what you need to spend your coins, therefore you are the only one who should hold it. You should keep your private key secure, preferably written down on paper and stored somewhere safe (like a safety deposit box). If your cryptocurrency is stored on an exchange, you likely won't have a private key and will use your exchange password to sell your coins.

2. Do not store your coins on an exchange long-term

No matter how good or reputable an exchange is, because of their centralized nature they are still vulnerable to being hacked. If you have any significant amount of cryptocurrency you should store it either in a desktop, paper or hardware wallet. For each of the coins listed I have provided links to wallets you can store them in. For hardware wallets I recommend the Trezor or Ledger Nano S, although not all coins are compatible with these.

3. Double check all links to websites (including ones in this book)

Phishing scams are still rife in the cryptocurrency space, and unfortunately, some of these links slip through Google Adwords checks and therefore appear at the top of a Google search for that cryptocurrency or exchange. Make sure you check the URL you are typing in or clicking on, so you don't end up on binnance.com or mynetherwallet.com by mistake. This is even more important when it's a website that requires your username and password.

4. **Don't reveal how much cryptocurrency you have**

I see this a lot on social media this days with people posting about their 5, 6 or even 7 figure portfolios. Your identity can be traced back to you if someone really wants to, and if they know you have millions of dollars worth of cryptocurrency, they suddenly have a motivation to do so. To be on the safe side, don't post on the internet regarding the amount of cryptocurrency you own. Posting about which coins you own is perfectly fine though.

5. **Get your news from reputable sources**

When investing in cryptocurrency, it can often be hard to know who to trust. There is a lot of misinformation out there, and this leads to bad investing moves. Unfortunately, mainstream media is particularly bad at reporting cryptocurrency news, preferring to choose soundbites that are attention-grabbing rather than fact-filled. For example, December saw articles stating "CEO of Bitcoin.com sells all his Bitcoin" but many of these articles failed to note that Bitcoin.com is merely a website that allows you to create Bitcoin wallets, and is no way an official Bitcoin operation. Which grossly overstated the event in the eyes of the general public.

I personally recommend cointelegraph.com and coindesk.com for keeping tabs on happenings within the cryptocurrency space.

Finally, never invest more than you can afford to lose, and never borrow money to invest in cryptocurrency.

Conclusion

Well there we have it, a summary of the cryptocurrency market and its direction as we head into 2018. As well as, a list of high potential coins that could have massive growth in the next 12 months and beyond. There has never been a better time to be involved in the world's fastest growing financial market, and if you haven't already invested, I hope this book gives you the confidence to do so.

Remember to only invest what you can afford to lose, and cryptocurrency investments should only make up a small percentage of your overall portfolio. I encourage you to do additional research before you invest your money, and remember to watch out for any nefarious elements like pump and dump schemes.

I wish you the best of luck in the cryptocurrency market, and I hope you make a lot of money.

Thanks,

Stephen

P.S. If you sign up for Coinbase using this link, you will receive $10 worth of free Bitcoin after your first purchase of more than $100 worth of cryptocurrency.

http://bit.ly/10dollarbtc

CPSIA information can be obtained
at www.ICGtesting.com
Printed in the USA
LVHW020510150221
679326LV00003B/140